JAVID NAMA

Translated from the Persian with
Introduction and Notes by

A.J. Arberry

SIR MUHAMMAD IQBAL

Qadeem Press

Qadeem Press

Qadeem Press Edition
Breathing Life into Forgotten Pages
www.qadeempress.com

Originally Published by George Allen & Unwin Ltd in 1966
Reprinted by Qadeem Press in 2025

CONTENTS

INTRODUCTION

The bare facts of the life and career of the author of the work here translated may be summarized in a few sentences; more extended biographies are not far to seek, and for the English-reading public A. Schimmel's *Gabriel's Wing*, Iqbal Singh's *The Passionate Pilgrim*, and S. A. Vahid's *Iqbal, his Art and Thought*, contain a wealth of detail and interpretation sufficient to satisfy the most exacting curiosity.

Muhammad Iqbal was born on February 22, 1873, at Sialkot, a populous centre of West Punjab near the borders of Jammu, of a family hailing originally from Kashmir. In 1895 he moved to Lahore to complete his formal studies, and there began to write. In 1905 on the advice of Sir Thomas Arnold, at that time teaching in Government College, he proceeded to England and for three years at Trinity College, Cambridge he applied his great energies chiefly to philosophy under McTaggart. Graduating from Cambridge in 1908, Iqbal qualified for the Bar in London and did post-graduate work in Germany before returning to India to teach in Lahore and to practise law; later he resigned his appointment at Government College and concentrated on his legal and political work. In 1924 he became a member of the Legislative Assembly of his native province, and in 1930 he was elected President of the Moslem League of India; meanwhile in 1922 a knighthood had been conferred upon him. Taking part in the London Round-Table Conference on India in 1931–32, he spent 1933 in Afghanistan as adviser on education. In 1934 his health began to decline, and on April 21, 1938, he died.

Throughout his extremely active life, in which he did so much to shape the destinies of the land of his birth and to mould the political future of the Moslem community (so that he has been called the spiritual founder of Pakistan), Iqbal maintained a steady and, towards the end, a torrential output of literature. Writing with equal facility in Urdu, Persian and English, and in his soaring range covering law, philosophy and religion as well as politics, it was as a poet that Iqbal made his greatest contribution to letters. On his death Rabindranath Tagore wrote: 'The death of Sir Muhammad Iqbal creates a void in literature that like a mortal wound will take a very long time to heal. India, whose place in the world is too narrow, can ill afford to miss a poet whose poetry had such universal value.' Iqbal's first publication, in 1901, was a treatise on economics in Urdu, the earliest to appear in that language; his last, issued posthumously under the title *Armughan-i Hijaz* ('Present from Hijaz'), contained his final collection of Persian and Urdu poems. The volume here translated, the *Javid-nama*, came out in 1932.

'Iqbal's *magnum opus*', writes his biographer S. A. Vahid, 'is the *Javid Namah*. Within a few years of its publication the poem became a classic, and one great scholar proclaimed that the poem will rank with Firdausi's *Shah Namah*, Rumi's *Mathnawi*, Sa'di's *Gulistan* and the *Diwan* of Hafiz. Nor was this tribute an exaggeration, as subsequent criticism showed . . . In judging a poem we have to consider two things: the style and the substance. So far as the style is concerned, *Javid Namah* belongs to the very first rank of Persian verse. It is unsurpassed in grandeur of expression, in beauty of diction and in richness of illustration. As regards theme, the poem deals with the everlasting conflict of the soul, and by telling the story of human struggle against sin, shows to mankind the path to glory and peace. In every line the poet makes us feel that he has something to say that is not only worth saying, but is also fitted to give us pleasure. Thus, as regards style as well as theme the poem is a masterpiece.'

The *Javid-nama*, having been frequently reissued in lithograph—the edition on which the present translation is based was published in 1946 at Hyderabad (Deccan)—was first translated, into Italian, by Professor Alessandro Bausani under the title *Il Poema Celeste* (Rome, 1952). A version in German verse, *Buch der Ewigkeit* (Munich, 1957), has come from the pen of Professor Annemarie Schimmel. A French version, by E. Meyerovitch and Mohammed Mokri, has the title *Le Livre de l'Éternité* (Paris, 1962). In 1961 a translation in English verse was published in Lahore, *The Pilgrimage of Eternity*, by Shaikh Mahmud Ahmad. The poem has thus reached a truly international public, and has already taken its rightful place amongst the modern classics of world literature.

Iqbal composed three long Persian poems in which he gave artistic expression to his highly characteristic philosophical ideas. The first of these, the *Asrar-i Khudi*, was published in 1915 and 'on its first appearance took by storm the younger generation of Indian Moslems. "Iqbal," wrote one of them, "has come amongst us as a Messiah and has stirred the dead into life."' So wrote R. A. Nicholson, whose prose version of this work, *The Secrets of the Self* (Macmillan, 1920), first introduced Iqbal's writings to the western public. The second of the trilogy, the *Rumuz-i Bekhudi*, came out in 1918, but it was not until 1953 that the first translation appeared, an English blank-verse rendering by the present writer entitled *The Mysteries of Selflessness* (John Murray).

As their titles indicate, the central theme of both these poems is the Self, or human ego, in its relationship to society, more specifically the Moslem community, and the place of the Moslem community in the world at large. In common with all sensitive Moslems in India and elsewhere, Iqbal was deeply pained by the contrast between Islam in the days of its greatest power, and the status of colonial tutelage—to use a mild euphemism—to which most Moslem countries had sunk in modern times. He saw the only hope of reversing the process of decline to reside in the regeneration of every individual Moslem, and the working together of these regenerated individuals in a united and purposeful Community of Believers, in God's good time coextensive with the whole of humanity. 'Thus the Kingdom of God on earth', Iqbal wrote in a famous letter to R. A. Nicholson, 'means the democracy of more or less unique individuals, presided over by the most unique individual possible on this earth.' For a developed philosophical exposition of his doctrine of the Self, in its maturest form, the reader is recommended to consult Iqbal's *Reconstruction of Religious Thought in Islam* (O.U.P., 1934), and especially chapter IV, 'The Human Ego—his freedom and immortality'.

Both the *Asrar-i khudi* and the *Rumuz-i bekhudi* were composed in rhyming couplets, following a very long tradition in Persian didactic poetry going back a thousand years. The metre chosen by Iqbal for these poems is the *ramal-i musaddas-i maqsur*, the same as that employed by the greatest of Persian mystics, Jalal al-Din Rumi (1207–1273), in the greatest didactic poem in

Persian literature, the *Masnavi*. I have summarized the early history of this verse-form in the preface to my *Tales from the Masnavi* (Allen & Unwin, 1961), which the reader may wish to consult. One noteworthy feature of the convention is that the poet lightens from time to time the weight of formal exposition by the introduction of illustrative anecdotes; to this tradition Iqbal also conformed. When, however, he came to compose the third of his trilogy, Iqbal varied the pattern strikingly; the *Javid-nama* is conceived as a narrative poem, or rather, a poetic drama, in which the didactic is put into the mouths of the *dramatis personae*. A further remarkable novelty is the interspersing of lyrics, in various metres and in the mono-rhyme characteristic of the Persian ghazal, the effect of which is a very great enhancement of the poetic tension of the whole.

The *Javid-nama* is a description of a spiritual journey made by the poet, from earth through the 'spheres' of the Moon, Mercury, Venus, Mars, Jupiter and Saturn, to beyond the 'spheres' and to the Presence of God. The antecedents of this heavenly adventure go back, within Islamic tradition, to the celebrated *mi'raj* of the Prophet Mohammed, that famous legend of his Ascension the germs of which are to be traced in the Koran. In his journey through the seven heavens Mohammed, mounted upon the winged horse Buraq, had as his guide the archangel Gabriel; in the course of his ascent he is said to have encountered and conversed with earlier prophets, from Adam in the first heaven to Abraham in the seventh, before enjoying the supreme felicity of colloquy with God. The Prophet's *mi'raj* naturally formed a theme of meditation and—as part of the *imitatio Prophetae*—of emulation for many pious Moslems and mystics through the succeeding centuries, and so Iqbal did not lack for precedents and models when he came to adopt this very popular vehicle for the final expression of his doctrine of Moslem regeneration and self-realization. He nominated as his guide the poet to whose language, style and thought he felt himself rightly to be under a special obligation, the Sage of Rum, Jalal al-Din Rumi; whilst the personalities he encountered on his journey were drawn not from the hierarchy of the prophets, but from those who had played a leading part in the history of Islam, particularly in its later period.

Iqbal presents the translator with all the usual problems connected with translating poetry, and with further problems, still more difficult of solution, posed by his elusive style and idiosyncratic vocabulary. That this elusiveness was deliberate is proved by a remark he jotted down in a notebook dating from 1910, and published by his son Javid in 1961: 'Matthew Arnold is a very precise poet. I like, however, an element of obscurity and vagueness in poetry; since the vague and the obscure appear profound to the emotions.' In choosing Persian as the medium for conveying his universal message, Iqbal was not adding materially to the difficulties of interpretation; rather the contrary, for Persian had been preferred by Indian Moslem poets for centuries over the local idioms, Persian being the court language of the Moghul Empire. (The rise of Urdu, and the consequent decline of the knowledge of Persian, in fact happened during Iqbal's lifetime; his own genius did very much to enhance its status and mature its style.) But Persian is a language almost ideally suited to deliberate vagueness, on account both of its grammatical and syntactical simplicity, and of its rich and at the same time somewhat imprecise philosophical vocabulary. Or rather, imprecision is not the crux of the matter; the case is, that the terms available for use are capable of a variety of meanings, and Iqbal, like every original thinker, not infrequently attached to quite simple words and clichés his own private signification.

This last point has been well made by S. A. Vahid in his *Iqbal, his Art and Thought*. 'The remarkable point about Iqbal's poetry is the sense of "newness," and the main reason for this is that although Iqbal was not actually anti-traditionalist, he uses certain words and combination of words to express his visions which are entirely original. Some of these words are coined by him; others represent old words used in an entirely new sense . . . He is also a superb phrase-maker and has wonderful felicity of phrasing by which language acquires meanings beyond those formally assigned by the lexicographer. These words and phrases act as the keystone for the entire arch of the poetic inspiration. As the removal of the keystone is sure to cause the downfall of the entire arch, so if we try to substitute something else for the master word or phrase, the whole artistic expression is marred . . . The use of those words and phrases give to Iqbal's poetry not only a sense of "newness" found in very few Urdu and Persian poets, but also the quality of surprise which characterises all great poetry.'

It has been said that the ideal at which the translator should aim is to produce a version as near as possible to what his original would have written, had he been composing in the translator's language and not his own. It so happens that in the case of the *Javid-nama*, we have been provided with material, though all too scanty, enabling us to test this theory; in his *Reconstruction of Religious Thought*, Iqbal has himself translated into English two passages from this poem. The first of these passages represents verses 2733–2736, which in Iqbal's own version become:

> The 'I am' which he seeketh,
> Lieth beyond philosophy, beyond knowledge.
> The plant which groweth only from the invisible soil of
> the heart of man,
> Groweth not from a mere heap of clay.

In the original Persian these lines read:

> *khvast ta az ab u gil ayad birun*
> *khusha-yi k-az kisht-i dil ayad birun*
> *anchi u juyad maqam-i kibriya-st*
> *in maqam az 'aql u hikmat ma-vara-st*

The poet thus not only reversed the original order of the two couplets, but also changed the tense of the main clause, itself in apposition to the immediately preceding sentence and having the same verbal construction, from the past to the present; nor, as will be seen, were these the only liberties he took with himself —liberties which would surely be condemned in any ordinary translator.

Iqbal's second self-translation is more extensive, representing lines 239 to 266 of the *Javid-nama*.

> Art thou in the stage of 'Life', 'death', or 'death-in-life'?
> Invoke the aid of three witnesses to verify thy 'Station'.
> The first witness is thine own consciousness—
> See thyself, then, with thine own light.
> The second witness is the consciousness of another ego—
> See thyself, then, with the light of an ego other than thee.
> The third witness is God's consciousness—
> See thyself, then, with God's light.

If thou standest unshaken in front of this light,
Consider thyself as living and eternal as He!
That man alone is real who dares—
Dares to see God face to face!
What is 'Ascension'? Only a search for a witness
Who may finally confirm thy reality—
A witness whose confirmation alone makes thee eternal.
No one can stand unshaken in His Presence;
And he who can, verily, he is pure gold.
Art thou a mere particle of dust?
Tighten the knot of thy ego;
And hold fast to thy tiny being!
How glorious to burnish one's ego
And to test its lustre in the presence of the Sun!
Re-chisel, then, thine ancient frame;
And build up a new being.
Such being is real being;
Or else thy ego is a mere ring of smoke!

The foregoing passage affords a very fair example of how close and how remote Iqbal was prepared to make his own version of himself; for comparison, in addition to the translation offered in the present volume, the reader may like to consider the verse-paraphrase by Shaikh Mahmud Ahmad.

Art thou alive or dead or dying fast?
Three witnesses should testify thy state.
The first as witness is the consciousness
Of self, to see thyself by thy own light.
The second is another's consciousness
That thou may'st kindle thus to see thyself.
And thy third witness is God's consciousness,
A light in which thou may'st see thyself.
Before the Lord's effulgence if thou stand'st
Thou art alive like Him. For life is but
To reach thy destined end, that is to see
The Lord unveiled. One who believes
Shall never lose himself in Attributes
For Mustafa insisted on the Sight.
The flight to heaven means a longing for
A witness who may testify thyself.

Unless it be confirmed by Him, our life
Is nothing but a play of tint and smell.
No one can stand against His beauty bright,
Except the one who has perfection reached.
O grain of sand! thy lustre do not lose,
Thy ego's knot but tighten up. Thy gleam
Increase, then test thyself against the sun,
If thou canst thus reshape thyself and pass
The test, thou art alive and praised or else
The fire of life is smoke and naught beside.

Other specimens of English versions of selected passages from the *Javid-nama* may be inspected in the general literature, by now extensive, which has developed out of studies of Iqbal. As for the translation here offered, the aim has been to adhere as closely as possible to the meaning of the original Persian; passages not immediately comprehensible, by reason of out-of-the-way references or otherwise, have been clarified in brief notes. Appended to the Persian text is an 'Address to Javid', the poet's son after whom the poem was named: this appendix does not form part of the whole work, and the present translator has followed the example of his predecessors and has omitted it.

TRANSLATION

DRAMATIS PERSONAE

RUMI, the Sage of Rum, Persian poet and mystic
ZARVAN, the Spirit of Time and Space
JAHAN-DOST, an Indian ascetic
SAROSH, a Mazdean angel
GAUTAMA, the Buddha
DANCING-GIRL
AHRIMAN, the Zoroastrian Principle of Evil
ZOROASTER
TOLSTOY
IFRANGIN, an embodiment of Europe
ABU JAHL, an enemy of the Prophet Mohammed
JAMAL AL-DIN AFGHANI, an Afghan religious reformer
SA'ID HALIM PASHA, a Turkish statesman and reformer
ZINDA-RUD, title bestowed on the author
MARDUKH, ancient idol
BAAL, ancient idol
PHARAOH
KITCHENER OF KHARTOUM
SUDANESE DERVISH, the Mahdi of Sudan
MARTIAN ASTRONOMER
MARTIAN PROPHETESS
HALLAJ, Persian mystic and martyr
GHALIB, Indian poet
QURRAT AL-AIN, Babi poetess and martyr
SATAN, a fallen angel called Iblis
SPIRIT OF INDIA
SADIQ, JAAFAR, Indian traitors
NIETZSCHE
SAYYID ALI HAMADANI, a Persian mystic known as Shah-i Hamadan

TAHIR GHANI, a poet of Kashmir
BARTARI-HARI, an ancient poet of India, Bhartrihari
NADIR, eighteenth century Shah of Persia
ABDALI, founder of modern Afghanistan, Ahmad Shah Durrani
NASIR-I KHUSRAU, an early Persian poet
MARTYR-KING, Tippoo Sultan of Mysore
HOURIS, maidens of Paradise
BEAUTY, an Aspect of God

PRAYER

Man, in this world of seven hues,
lute-like is ever afire with lamentation;
yearning for a kindred spirit burns him inwardly
teaching him threnodies to soothe the heart,
and yet this world, that is wrought of water and clay—
how can it be said to possess a heart?
Sea, plain, mountain, grass—all are deaf and dumb,
deaf and dumb heaven and sun and moon;
though the stars swarm in the selfsame sky
each star is more solitary than the other,
each one is desperate just as we are,
a vagrant lost in an azure wilderness—
the caravan unprovisioned against the journey,
the heavens boundless, the nights interminable.
Is this world then some prey, and we the huntsmen,
or are we prisoners utterly forgotten?
Bitterly I wept, but echo answered never:
where may Adam's son find a kindred spirit?

I have seen that the day of this dimensioned world
whose light illuminates both palace and street
came into being from the flight of a planet,
is nothing more, you might say, than a moment gone.
How fair is the Day that is not of our days,
the Day whose dawn has neither noon nor eve!
Let its light illuminate the spirit
and sounds become visible even as colours;
hidden things become manifest in its splendour,
its watch is unending and intransient.
Grant me that Day, Lord, even for a single day,
deliver me from this day that has no glow!

Concerning whom was the Verse of Subjection revealed?
For whose sake spins the azure sphere so wildly?
Who was it knew the secret of *He taught the names?*
Who was intoxicated with that saki and that wine?
Whom didst Thou choose out of all the world?
To whom didst Thou confide the innermost secret?
O Thou whose arrow transpierced our breast,
who uttered the words *Call upon me*, and to whom?
Thy countenance is my faith, and my Koran:
dost Thou begrudge my soul one manifestation?
By the loss of a hundred of its rays
the sun's capital is in no wise diminished.

Reason is a chain fettering this present age:
where is a restless soul such as I possess?
For many ages Being must twist on itself
that one restless soul may come into being.
Except you fret away at this brackish soil
it is not congenial to the seed of desire;
count it for gain enough if a single heart
grows from the bosom of this unproductive clay!
Thou art a moon: pass within my dormitory,
glance but once on my unenlightened soul.
Why does the flame shrink away from the stubble?
Why is the lightning-flash afraid to strike?

So long as I have lived, I have lived in separation:
reveal what lies beyond yon azure canopy;
open the doors that have been closed in my face,
let earth share the secrets of heaven's holy ones.
Kindle now a fire within my breast—
leave be the aloe, and consume the brushwood,
then set my aloe again upon the fire
and scatter my smoke through all the world.
Stir up the fire within my goblet,
mingle one glance with this inadvertency.

We seek Thee, and Thou art far from our sight;
no, I have erred—we are blind, and Thou art present.
Either draw aside this veil of mysteries
or seize to Thyself this sightless soul!
The date-tree of my thought despairs of leaf and fruit;
either despatch the axe, or the breeze of dawn.
Thou gavest me reason, give me madness too,
show me the way to inward ecstasy.
Knowledge takes up residence in the thought,
love's lodge is the unsleeping heart;
so long as knowledge has no portion of love
it is a mere picture-gallery of thoughts.
This peep-show is the Samiri's conjuring-trick;
knowledge without the Holy Ghost is mere spellbinding.
Without revelation no wise man ever found the way,
he died buffetted by his own imaginings;
without revelation life is a mortal sickness,
reason is banishment, religion constraint.
This world of mountain and plain, ocean and land—
we yearn for vision, and it speaks of report.
Grant to this vagrant heart a resting-place,
restore to the moon this fragment of the moon.
Though from my soil nothing grows but words,
the language of banishment never comes to an end.
Under the heavens I feel myself a stranger:
from beyond the skies utter the words *I am near*,
that these dimensions, this north and this south,
like to the sun and moon in the end may set,
I shall transcend the talisman of yesterday
and tomorrow, transcend the moon, sun, Pleiades.

Thou art eternal splendour; we are like sparks—
a breath or two we possess, and that too borrowed.
You who know naught of the battle of death and life,
who is this slave who would emulate even God?
This slave, impatient, conquering all horizons,
finds pleasure neither in absence nor in presence.
I am a momentary thing: make me eternal,

out of my earthiness make me celestial.
Grant me precision both in speech and action:
the ways are clear— give me the strength to walk.
What I have said comes from another world;
this book descends from another heaven.
I am a sea; untumult in me is a fault;
where is he who can plunge into my depths?
A whole world slumbered upon my shore
and saw from the strand naught but the surge of a wave.
I, who despair of the great sages of old,
have a word to say touching the day to come!
Render my speech easy unto the young,
make my abyss for them attainable.

PRELUDE IN HEAVEN

On the first day of creation Heaven rebukes Earth

Life out of the delight of absence and presence
fashioned forth this world of near and far;
so snapped asunder the thread of the moment
and mixed the hues of Time's house of amazement.
On all sides, out of the joyous yearning for habitude
arose the cry: 'I am one thing, you are another.'
The moon and the stars learned the way to walk,
a hundred lamps were kindled in the firmament.
In the azure heavens the sun pitched
its gold-cloth tent with its silver ropes,
raised its head over the rim of the first dawn
and drew to its breast the new-born world.
Man's realm was a heap of earth, no more,
an empty wilderness, without a caravan;
not a river wrestled in any mountain,
not a cloud sprinkled on any desert,
no chanting of birds among the branches,
no leaping of deer amidst the meadow.
Sea and land lacked the spirit's manifestations,
a curling vapour was the mantle of earth's body;
the grasses, never having known the breeze of March,
still slumbered within the depths of earth.
The azure sky then chided the earth, saying:
'I never saw anyone pass so miserable a life!
In all my breadth what creature is so blind as you?
What light is yours, save that drawn from my lamp?
Be earth high as Alvand, yet it is only earth,
it is not bright and eternal as the skies.
Either live with the apparatus of a heart-charmer,
or die of the shame and misery of worthlessness!'

Earth felt put to shame by heaven's reproach,
desperate, heavy of heart, utterly annihilated,
fluttered before God in the agony of unlight.
Suddenly a voice echoed from beyond the skies:
'O trusty one, as yet unaware of the trust,
be not sorrowful; look within thy own heart.
The days are bright of the tumult of life,
not through the light thou seest spread in all quarters.
Dawn's light comes from the spotted sun,
the soul's light is unsullied by the dust of time;
the soul's light is upon a pathless journey,
roves farther than the rays of sun and moon.
Thou hast washed from the soul's tablet the image of hope,
yet the soul's light manifests out of thy dust!
Man's reason is making assault on the world,
but his love makes assault on the Infinite;
his thought knows the way without any guide,
his sight is more wakeful than Gabriel.
Earthy, yet in flight he is like an angel;
heaven is but an ancient inn upon his way;
he pricks into the very depths of the heavens
like the point of a needle into silk;
he washes the stains from the skirt of Being,
and without his glance, the world is blank and blind.
Though few his magnificats, and much blood he sheds,
yet he is as a spur in the flanks of doom.
His sight becomes keen through observing phenomena
so that he sees the Essence within the attributes.
Whoever falls in love with the beauty of Essence,
he is the master of all existing things.'

Song of the Angels

The lustre of a handful of earth one day shall outshine the
creatures of light;
earth through the star of his destiny one day shall be
transformed into heaven.
His imagination, which is nourished by the torrent of
vicissitudes,

one day shall soar out of the whirlpool of the azure sky.
Consider one moment the meaning of Man; what thing do you ask of us?
Now he is pricking into nature, one day he will be modulated perfectly,
so perfectly modulated will this precious subject be
that even the heart of God will bleed one day at the impact of it!

PRELUDE ON EARTH

The Spirit of Rumi appears and explains the mystery of the Ascension

Tumultuous love, indifferent to the city—
for in the city's clangour its flame dies—
seeks solitude in desert and mountain-range
or on the shore of an unbounded sea.
I, who saw among my friends none to confide in,
rested a moment on the shore of the sea:
the sea, and the hour of the setting sun—
the blue water was a liquid ruby in the gloaming.
Sunset gives to the blind man the joy of sight,
sunset gives to evening the hue of dawn.
I held conversation with my heart;
I had many desires, many requests—
a thing of the moment, unsharing immortality,
a thing living, unsharing life itself,
thirsty, and yet far from the rim of the fountain,
involuntarily I chanted this song.

Ghazal

Open your lips, for abundant sugar-candy is my desire;
show your cheek, for the garden and rosebed are my desire.
In one hand a flask of wine, in the other the beloved's tress—
such a dance in the midst of the maidan is my desire.
You said, 'Torment me no more with your coquetry: begone!'
That saying of yours, 'Torment me no more,' is my desire.
O reason, become out of yearning a babbler of words confused;

O love, distracted subtleties are my desire.
This bread and water of heaven are fickle as a torrent;
I am a fish, a leviathan—Oman is my desire.
My soul has grown aweary of Pharaoh and his tyranny;
that light in the breast of Moses, Imran's son, is my desire.
Last night the Elder wandered about the city with a lantern
saying, 'I am weary of demon and monster: man is my desire.'
My heart is sick of these feeble-spirited fellow-travellers;
the Lion of God and Rustam-i Dastan, are my desire.
I said, 'The thing we quested after is never attained.'
He said, 'The unattainable—that thing is my desire!'

The restless wave slept on the grey water,
the sun vanished, dark grew the horizon—
evening stole a portion of its capital
and a star stood like a witness above the roof.
The spirit of Rumi rent the veils asunder;
from behind a mountain mass he became visible,
his face shining like the sun in splendour,
his white hairs radiant as the season of youth—
a figure bright in a light immortal,
robed from head to foot in everlasting joy.
Upon his lips the hidden secret of Being
loosed from itself the chains of speech and sound:
his speech was as a suspended mirror,
knowledge commingled with an inward fire.
I asked him, 'What is the existent, the non-existent?
What is the meaning of praiseworthy and unpraiseworthy?'
He said, 'The existent is that which wills to appear:
manifestation is all the impulse of Being.
Life means to adorn oneself in one's self,
to desire to bear witness to one's own being;
the concourse on the day primordial arrayed
desired to bear witness to their own being.
Whether you be alive, or dead, or dying—
for this seek witness from three witnesses.
The first witness is self-consciousness,

to behold oneself in one's own light;
the second witness is the consciousness of another,
to behold oneself in another's light;
the third witness is the consciousness of God's essence,
to behold oneself in the light of God's essence.
If you remain fast before this light,
count yourself living and abiding as God!
Life is to attain one's own station,
life is to see the Essence without a veil;
the true believer will not make do with Attributes—
the Prophet was not content save with the Essence.
What is Ascension? The desire for a witness,
an examination face-to-face of a witness—
a competent witness without whose confirmation
life to us is like colour and scent to a rose.
In that Presence no man remains firm,
or if he remains, he is of perfect assay.
Give not away one particle of the glow you have,
knot tightly together the glow within you;
fairer it is to increase one's glow,
fairer it is to test oneself before the sun;
then chisel anew the crumbled form;
make proof of yourself; be a true being!
Only such an existent is praiseworthy,
otherwise the fire of life is mere smoke.'

I asked again, 'How shall one go before God?
How may one split the mountain of clay and water?
The Orderer and Creator is outside Order and Creation;
we—our throats are strangled by the noose of Fate.'
He said, 'If you obtain the Authority
you can break through the heavens easily.
Wait till the day creation all is naked
and has washed from its skirt the dust of dimension;
then you will see neither waxing nor waning in its being,
you will see yourself as of it, and it of you.
Recall the subtlety *Except with an authority*
or die in the mire like an ant or a locust!

It was by way of birth, excellent man,
that you came into this dimensioned world;
by birth it is possible also to escape,
it is possible to loosen all fetters from oneself;
but such a birth is not of clay and water—
that is known to the man who has a living heart.
The first birth is by constraint, the second by choice;
the first is hidden in veils, the second is manifest;
the first happens with weeping, the second with laughter,
for the first is a seeking, the second a finding;
the first is to dwell and journey amidst creation,
the second is utterly outside all dimensions;
the first is in need of day and night,
the second—day and night are but its vehicle.
A child is born through the rending of the womb,
a man is born through the rending of the world;
the call to prayer signalizes both kinds of birth,
the first is uttered by the lips, the second of the very soul.
Whenever a watchful soul is born in a body
this ancient inn, the world, trembles to its foundations!'

I said, 'I know not what manner of birth this is.'
He said, 'It is one of the high estates of life.
Life plays at vanishing and then reappearing—
one role is constant, the other transitory;
now life dissolves itself in manifestation,
anon it concentrates itself in solitude.
Its manifestation shines with the light of the Attributes,
its solitude is lit up by the light of the Essence.
Reason draws life towards manifestation,
love draws life towards solitude.
Reason likewise hurls itself against the world
to shatter the talisman of water and clay;
every stone on the road becomes its preceptor,
lightning and cloud preach sermons to it.
Its eye is no stranger to the joy of seeing,
but it possesses not the drunkard's boldness;
therefore, fearing the road, it gropes like a blind man,

softly, gently it creeps along, just like an ant.
So long as reason is involved with colour and scent
slowly it proceeds upon the path to the Beloved;
its affairs achieve some order gradually—
I do not know when they will ever be completed!
Love knows nothing of months and years,
late and soon, near and far upon the road.
Reason drives a fissure through a mountain,
or else makes a circuit around it;
before love the mountain is like a straw,
the heart darts as swiftly as a fish.
Love means, to make assault upon the Infinite,
without seeing the grave to flee the world.
Love's strength is not of air and earth and water,
its might derives not from toughness of sinew;
love conquered Khaibar on a loaf of barley,
love clove asunder the body of the moon,
broke Nimrod's cranium without a blow,
without a battle shattered Pharaoh's hosts.
Love in the soul is like sight in the eye,
be it within the house or without the door;
love is at once both ashes and spark,
its work is loftier than religion and science.
Love is authority and manifest proof,
both worlds are subject to the seal-ring of love;
timeless it is, and yesterday and tomorrow spring from it,
placeless it is, and under and over spring from it;
when it supplicates God for selfhood
all the world becomes a mount, itself the rider.
Through love, the heart's status becomes clearer;
through love, the draw of this ancient inn becomes void.
Lovers yield themselves up to God,
give interpretative reason as an offering.
Are you a lover? Proceed from direction to directionless-
ness;
make death a thing prohibited to yourself.
You who are like a dead man in the grave's coffer,
resurrection is possible without the sound of the Trumpet!
You have in your throat melodies sweet and delicate;
how long will you croak like a frog in the mud?

Boldly ride upon space and time,
break free of the convolutions of this girdle;
sharpen your two eyes and your two ears—
whatever you see, digest by way of the understanding.
"The man who hears the voice of the ants
also hears from Time the secret of Fate."
Take from me the glance that burns the veil,
the glance that becomes not the eye's prisoner.
"Man is but sight, the rest is mere skin;
true sight signifies seeing the Beloved.
Dissolve the whole body into sight—
go to gazing, go to gazing, go to gaze!"
Are you afraid of these nine heavens? Fear not;
are you afraid of the world's immensity? Fear not.
Open wide your eyes upon Time and Space,
for these two are but a state of the soul.
Since first the gaze advanced on manifestation
the alternation of yesterday and tomorrow was born.
The seed lying in the soil's house of darkness
a stranger to the vast expanse of the sky—
does it not know that in an ample space
it can display itself, branch by branch.
What is its substance? A delight in growing;
this substance is both its station and itself.

You who say that the body is the soul's vehicle,
consider the soul's secret; tangle not with the body.
It is not a vehicle, it is a state of the soul;
to call it its vehicle is a confusion of terms.
What is the soul? Rapture, joy, burning and anguish,
delight in mastering the revolving sphere.
What is the body? Habit of colour and scent,
habit of dwelling in the world's dimensions.
Your near and far spring out of the senses;
what is Ascension? A revolution in sense,
a revolution in sense born of rapture and yearning;
rapture and yearning liberate from under and over.
This body is not the associate of the soul;
a handful of earth is no impediment to flight.'

Zarvan, the Spirit of Time and Space, conducts the Traveller on his journey to the Supernal World

My soul was convulsed by the words that he spoke,
every atom of my body trembled like quicksilver.
Suddenly I saw, between the West and the East,
heaven immersed in a single cloud of light;
out of that cloud an angel descended
having two faces, one like fire, one like smoke—
one dark as night, the other bright as a meteor,
the eyes of one watchful, the other's eyes asleep.
The hues of his wings were of crimson and gold,
emerald and silver, azure and lapis-lazuli;
his temper had the fleetness even of a phantom,
he sped from earth to the Milky Way in an instant;
every moment he was seized by another desire,
to spread his wings in yet another sky.
He said, 'I am Zarvan, I am the world-subduer,
alike hidden from sight and manifest am I.
Every plan is bound up with my determining;
voiced and voiceless—all alike are my prey.
Through me the bud swells upon the branch,
through me the birdie bewails in the nest;
through my flight the seed becomes a stalk,
through my effluence every parting turns to union.
I pronounce both reproach and exhortation;
I render athirst, that I may offer wine.
I am life, I am death, I am resurrection,
I am the Judgment, Hell, Heaven and Houri.
Man and angel are both in bondage to me,
this transitory world is my own child;
I am every rose that you pluck from the branch,
I am the matrix of every thing that you see.
This world is a prisoner in my talisman,
every moment it ages through my breath.
But he who has in his heart *I have a time with God*,
that doughty hero has broken my talisman;
if you wish that I should not be in the midst,
recite from the depths of your soul *I have a time with God*.'

I know not what it was that was in his glance,
it snatched away from my sight this ancient world;
either my sight opened on another world
or this same world took on another form.
I died in the universe of colour and scent,
I was born in a world without tumult and clamour;
my thread snapped from that ancient world,
a whole new world came into my hands.
My soul trembled at the loss of a world
until another world blossomed out of my dust;
my body became nimbler, my soul more adventurous,
the eye of my heart was keener and more wakeful;
veiled things became manifest uncurtained,
the melody of the stars reached my ears.

Chant of the Stars

Your reason is the fruit of life, your love is creation's mystery;
O form of dust, welcome to this side of the world of dimensions!
Venus and Moon and Jupiter are rivals on your account,
for one glance from you there's a great jostle of manifestations.
On the road to the Beloved there are revelations ever fresh and new;
the man of true yearning and desire yields not his heart to the All.
Life is truth and purity, life is quickening and surging;
gallop from eternity to eternity; life is the Kingdom of God.
Unto the passion of minstrelsy give leave to clamour and riot,
give wine again to profligate and censor, wine pitcher on pitcher.
Syria and Iraq, India and Persia are accustomed to the sugar-cane;
give to the sugar-cane's habituate the bitterness of desire!

That it may enter upon battle with the high-billowed ocean
give to the heart of the rivulet the joy of the swift torrent.
The poor man is a fire, rulership and power imperial are straw;
a naked sword is ample enough for the august pomp of kings.
The drumming of the dervish, Alexander's clamorous vanity—
the one is the rapture of Moses, the other the Samiri's conjuring.
The one slays with a glance, the other slays with an army;
the one is all peace and amity, the other is all war and wrangling.
Both were conquerors of the world, both sought immortality,
the one by the guidance of violence, the other guided by love.
Bring the hammer-blow of the dervish, break the rampart of Alexander;
renew the ancient wont of Moses, break the glamour of wizardry!

THE SPHERE OF THE MOON

This earth and heaven are the Kingdom of God,
this moon and Pleiades are our patrimony;
whatever thing meets your gaze upon this road,
regard it with the eye of intimacy.
Go not about your own dwelling like a stranger—
you who are lost to yourself, be a little fearless!
This and that impose your command on their hearts;
if you say 'Don't do this, do that,' they obey.
The world is nothing but idols of eye and ear;
its every morrow will die like yesterday.
Plunge like a madman into the desert of the Quest,
that is to say, be the Abraham of this idol-house!
When you have travelled all through earth and heaven,
when you have traversed this world and the other,
seek from God another seven heavens,
seek a hundred other times and spaces.
Self-lost to sink on the bank of the river of Paradise,
quit of the battle and buffetting of good and evil—
if our salvation be the cessation of searching,
better the grave than a heaven of colours and scents.
Traveller! the soul dies of dwelling at rest,
it becomes more alive by perpetual soaring.
Delightful it is to travel along with the stars,
delightful not to rest one moment on the journey.
When I had tramped through the vastness of space
that which was once above now appeared below me,
a dark earth loftier than the lamp of night,
my shadow (O marvel!) flung above my head;
all the while nearer and nearer still
until the mountains of the Moon became visible.
Rumi said, 'Cleanse yourself of all doubts,
grow used to the manners and ways of the spheres.
The moon is far from us, yet it is our familiar;
this is the first stage upon our road;

seen must be the late and soon of its time,
seen must be the caverns of its mountains.'

That silence, that fearful mountain-range,
inwardly full of fire, outwardly riven and ravined!
A hundred peaks, such as Khaftin and Yildirim,
smoke in their mouths and fire in their bellies;
out of its bosom not a blade of grass sprang,
no bird fluttered in its empty spaces;
clouds without moisture, winds swift and sword-sharp
ever doing battle with a dead earth.
A worn-out world without colour and sound,
no sign of life therein, neither of death,
no root of the palm-tree of life in its navel,
no events hidden in the thighs of its time;
though it is a member of the family of the sun
its dawn and evening beget no revolution.

Rumi said, 'Rise, and take a step forward,
do not let slip this wakeful fortune.
Its interior is fairer than its exterior,
another world lurks hidden in its hollows.
Whatever presents itself to you, man of sense,
seize it in the rings of the eye and the ear.
If the eye has vision, everything is worth seeing,
worthy to be weighed in the glance's balance.
Wheresoever Rumi leads, there go;
be estranged a moment or two from all but he.'
Gently he drew my hand towards him,
then swiftly he sped to the mouth of a crater.

An Indian ascetic, known to the people of India as Jahan-Dost, who lives as a hermit in one of the caverns of the moon

Like a blind man, my hand on my companion's shoulder,
I placed my foot within a deep cavern;
the moon's heart was sore ravaged by its darkness,

within it even the sun would have needed a lamp.
Fancies and doubts made assault upon me,
hung my reason and sense upon the gallows.
I went along a road where highwaymen lurked in ambush,
my heart void of the joy of truth and certainty;
presently manifestations met my gaze unveiled,
a bright dawn without any rising of the sun—
a valley, whereof each stone was an idolater,
a demon's haunt thick with lofty palm-trees.
Was this place truly compounded of earth and water,
or was my sleeping fantasy painting pictures?
The air was filled with the joy and gaiety of wine,
the shadows, kissing its dust, were light's own essence.
No cerulean sky spanned its earth,
no twilight painted its margin crimson and gold;
there light was not in the chains of darkness,
there no mists enveloped dawn and eventide.
Under a palm-tree an Indian sage,
the pupils of his eyes bright with collyrium,
his hair knotted on his head, his body naked,
coiled about him a white snake writhing,
a man superior to water and clay,
the world a mere image in the cloister of his fantasy,
his time subject to no revolution of days,
he had no traffick with the azure-tinted skies.
He said to Rumi, 'Who is your fellow-traveller?
In his glance there is a desire for life!'

Rumi

A man who is a wanderer on the quest,
a fixed star with the constitution of a planet.
His enterprise is more mature than his immaturities;
I am a martyr to his imperfections.
He has made of his glass the arch of heaven,
his thought seeks to be boon-companion of Gabriel!
He swoops like an eagle on the moon and sun, his prey,
hot-foot he circumambulates the nine spheres.

A drunkard's words he has spoken to the people of earth
calling the houris idols, Paradise an idol-house.
I have seen flames in the billow of his smoke,
I have seen majestic pride in his prostration.
Ever he laments yearningly like a flute,
separation and union alike slay him.
I do not know what is in his water and clay;
I do not know what his rank and station may be.

Jahan-Dost

The world is a thing of colour, and God is without colour.
What is the world? What is man? What is God?

Rumi

Man is a sword, and God is the swordsman;
the world is the whetstone for this sword.
The East saw God and did not see the world,
the West crept along the world and fled away from God.
True servanthood is to open the eyes to God;
true life is to see oneself without a veil.
When a servant takes quittance of life
God Himself calls down blessings on that servant.
Whatever man is unconscious of his destiny,
his dust travels not with the fire of the soul.

Jahan-Dost

Tied up in the knot of being and not-being
the East has seen little into these secrets.
The task of us celestials is only to see,
and my soul does not despair of the East's tomorrow.
Yesterday I saw on the summit of Qashmarud
an angel that had descended out of heaven;
out of his glance the joy of sight distilled
as he gazed solely towards our mound of dust.
I said to him, 'Hide not a secret from your confidants;

what is it that you see in this silent dust?
Do you melt for the beauty of some Venus?
Have you flung your heart into the well of Babylon?'
He said, 'It is the hour of the East's arising;
the East has a new sun shining in its breast.
Rubies come forth from the stones of the road,
its Josephs are issuing out of the well.
I have seen a resurrection happening in its bloom,
I have seen its mountains trembling and quaking;
it is packing up to quit the station of Azar
at last to forswear forever idolatry.
Happy is the people whose soul has fluttered,
that has created itself anew out of its own clay.
For the Throne-angels that hour is the dawn of festival
when the eyes of a nation at last awake!'

The Indian sage was silent for a little while;
then he looked at me again, somewhat impatiently.
He asked, 'Death of the reason?' I said, 'Giving up thought.'
He asked, 'Death of the heart?' I said, 'Giving up remembrance.'
He asked, 'The body?' I said, 'Born of the dust of the road.'
He asked, 'The Soul?' I said, 'The symbol of One God.'
He asked, 'And Man?' I said, 'One of God's secrets.'
He asked, 'The world?' I said, 'Itself stands face to face.'
He asked, 'This science and art?' I said, 'Mere husk.'
He asked, 'What is the proof?' I said, 'The face of the Beloved.'
He asked, 'The commons' religion?' I said, 'Just hearsay.'
He asked, 'The gnostics' religion?' I said, 'True seeing.'
My words brought much pleasure to his soul,
and he disclosed to me delightful subtleties.

Nine sayings of the Indian sage

This world is not a veil over the Essence of God;
the image in the water is no barrier to plunging in.

2

It is delightful to be born into another world,
so that another youth may thereby be attained.

3

God is beyond death, He is the very essence of life;
when His servant dies, He knows not what is happening.
Though we are birds without wings or feathers,
we know more of the science of death than God.

4

Time? It is a sweet mingled with poison,
a general compassion mingled with vengeance;
you see neither city nor plain free of its vengeance—
its compassion is that you may say, 'It has passed.'

5

Unbelief is death, my enlightened friend;
how beseems it a hero to wage holy war on the dead?
The believer is living, and at war with himself,
he falls upon himself like a panther on a deer.

6

The infidel with a wakeful heart praying to an idol
is better than a religious man asleep in the sanctuary.

7

Blind is the eye that sees sin and error;
never does the sun behold the night.

8

Association with the mire makes the seed a tree;
man by association with the mire is brought to shame.
The seed receives from the mire twisting and turning
that it may make its prey the rays of the sun.

9

I said to the rose, 'Tell me, you with your torn breast,
how do you take colour and scent from the wind and the dust?'
The rose said, 'Intelligent man bereft of intelligence,

how do you take a message from the silent electric ray?
The soul is in our body through the attraction of this and that;
your attraction is manifest, whereas ours is hidden.'

Epiphany of Sarosh

Thereupon the wise man ceased his discourse;
self-intoxicated, he broke away from the world—
ecstasy and yearning snatched him out of his own hands.
Then came into being, by the magic of divine vision—
when it is present the motes become like Mount Sinai,
without its presence there is nor light nor manifestation—
a delicate creature in the talisman of that night,
a star shining upon that starless night.
The hyacinth-curls of his two tresses reached his waist,
mountains and foothills drew brilliance from his face.
Wholly drowned in a drunken epiphany,
drunken without wine, he chanted melodiously.
Before him the lantern of the imagination span around,
full of wiles as the ancient sphere of heaven;
in that lantern appeared a form of many hues,
hawk pouncing on sparrow, panther seizing deer.
I said to Rumi, 'You who know the secret,
reveal the secret to your companion of little vision.'
He said, 'This form like unto flashing silver
was born in the thought of the holy God;
impatiently, out of the joy of self-manifestation,
he came down into the dormitory of existence,
like ourselves a wanderer, exile his portion—
you are an exile, I am an exile, he is an exile.
His rank is that of Gabriel, his name is Sarosh,
he transports from sense, and restores to sense.
It was his dew that opened our bud,
the fire of his breath kindled the dead ember.
The poet's plectrum striking the chords of the heart is of him,
and it is he who rends the veil shrouding the Kaaba.

Within his melody I have glimpsed an entire universe:
now take fire for a moment from his song.'

The Song of Sarosh

I fear that you are steering the barque into a mirage;
born within a veil, you will die within a veil.
When I washed the collyrium of Razi from my eyes
I saw the destinies of nations hidden in the Book.
Twist over field and avenue, twist over mountain and desert—
the lightning that twists upon itself dies within the cloud.
I dwelt a while with the Westerners, sought much and saw scarcely
the man whose musical modes turn not upon number.
Without the anguish of battle that propinquity is not attainable;
you who speak of 'scent in rose-water,' go, ravish the rose-bush!

Superficial ascetic, I concede that selfhood is transient,
but you do not see the whirlpool within the bubble.
This delightful music comes not from the minstrel's plucking,
a houri exiled from Paradise is weeping within the lute.

Departure for the Valley of Yarghamid, called by the Angels the Valley of Tawasin

Rumi, that guide to passion and love
whose words are as Salsabil to throats athirst,
said, 'The poetry in which there is fire
originates from the heat of "He is God!"
That chant transforms rubbish into a rose-garden,
that chant throws into confusion the spheres,
that chant bears testimony to the Truth,
bestows on beggars the rank of kings.
Through it the blood courses swifter in the body,
the heart grows more aware of the Trusty Spirit.

Many a poet through the magic of his art
is a highwayman of hearts, a devil of the glance.
The poet of India—God help him,
and may his soul lack the joy of speech!—
has taught love to become a minstrel,
taught the friends of God the art of Azar.
His words are a sparrow's chirp, no ardour or anguish;
the people of passion call him a corpse, not a man.
Sweeter than that sweet chant which knows no mode
are the words which you utter in a dream.
The poet's nature is all searching,
creator and nourisher of desire;
the poet is like the heart in a people's breast,
a people without a poet is a mere heap of clay.
Ardour and drunkenness embroider a world;
poetry without ardour and drunkenness is a dirge.
If the purpose of poetry is the fashioning of men,
poetry is likewise the heir of prophecy.'

I said, 'Speak again also of prophecy,
speak again its secret to your confidant.'
He said, 'Peoples and nations are his signs,
our centuries are things of his creation.
His breath makes stones and bricks to speak;
we all are as the harvest, he the sown field.
He purifies the bones and fibres,
gives to the thoughts the wings of Gabriel;
the mutterings within the hearts of creatures
upon his lip become *Star*, *Light*, and *Pluckers*.
To his sun there is no setting, none;
to his denier never shall come perfection.
God's compassion is the company of his freemen,
the wrath of God is his impetuous blow.
Be you Universal Reason itself, flee not from him,
for he beholds both body and soul together.
Stride then more nimbly on the road to Yarghamid
that you may see that which must be seen—
engraved upon a wall of moonstone
behold the four Tasins of prophecy.'

Yearning knows its own way without a guide,
the yearning to fly with the wings of Gabriel;
for yearning the long road becomes two steps,
such a traveller wearies of standing still.
As if drunk I strode out towards Yarghamid
until at last its heights became visible.
What shall I say of the splendour of that station?
Seven stars circle about it unceasingly;
the Carpet-angels are inly lit by its light,
its dust's collyrium brightens the eyes of the Throne-angels.
God gave to me sight, heart and speech,
gave me the urge to search for the world of secrets;
now I will unveil the mysteries of the universe,
I will tell you of the Tawasin of the Apostles.

TASIN OF GAUTAMA

The Repentance of the coquettish Dancing-Girl

Gautama

Ancient wine and youthful beloved are—nothing;
for men of true vision the houris of Paradise are—nothing.
Whatever you know as firm and enduring passes away,
mountain and desert, land, sea and shore are—nothing.
The science of the Westerners, the philosophy of the Easterners
are all idol-houses, and the visiting of idols yields—nothing.
Think upon Self, and pass not fearfully through this desert,
for you are, while the substance of both worlds is—nothing.
On the road which I hewed out with the point of my eyelash
station and caravan and shifting sands are—nothing.

Transcend the unseen, for this doubt and surmise are nothing;
to be in the world and to escape from the world—that is something!
The Paradise that some God grants unto you is nothing;

when Paradise is the reward of your labours—that is something.
Do you seek repose for your soul? The soul's repose is nothing;
the tear shed in sorrow for your companions—that is something.
The wine-drenched eye, the temptress glance and the song
are all fair, but sweeter than these—there is something.
The cheek's beauty lives for a moment, in a moment is no more;
the beauty of action and fine ideals—that is something.

The Dancing-Girl

Give not occasion for conturbation to this restless heart;
add one or two curls more to my twisted tress.
In my breast is such a lightning-flash of revelation from you,
I have yielded the bitterness of expectation to the moon and the sun.
The joy of God's presence founded in this world idolatry's wont;
love ever eludes the soul that is full of hope.
So that with carefree heart I may play a new melody
give back again to the meadow the true bird of the meadow.
You have granted me a lofty nature; release the shackle from my foot
that I may bestow a prince's robe upon your sackcloth.
If the axe struck against the stone, what cause of talk is that?
Love can carry upon its back a whole mountain-range!

TASIN OF ZOROASTER

Ahriman Tempts Zoroaster

Ahriman

Because of you my creatures complain like a reed-pipe,
because of you our April has become like December;
you have made me humbled and dishonoured in the world,

you have stained your image with my blood.
Truth lives through the epiphany of your Sinai,
death for me dwells within your White Hand.

It is folly to rely on a covenant with God,
to travel the road to His desire is to lose the way;
poisons lurk within His rose-tinted wine.
saw, worm and cross—these are His gifts.
Noah had no other resource but prayer,
but the words of that hapless man were of no avail.
So abandon the city and hide yourself in a cave,
choose the company of the cavalcade of the creatures of light;
with one glance make the dust a philosopher's stone,
set fire to the heavens with a single prayer;
become a wanderer in the mountains like Moses,
be half-consumed in the fire of vision;
but you must certainly give up prophecy,
you must give up all such mullah-mongery.
By associating with nobodies, a somebody becomes a nobody,
though his nature be a flame, he becomes a chip of wood.
So long as prophethood is inferior to sainthood
prophecy is a veritable vexation to love.
Now rise, and nestle in the nest of Unity,
abandon manifestation and sit in retirement!

Zoroaster

Light is the ocean, darkness is but its shore;
no torrent like me was ever born in its heart.
My breast is swarming with restless waves;
what should the torrent do but devastate the shore?
The colourless picture, which no man has ever seen,
cannot be painted save with the blood of Ahriman.
Self-display—that is the very secret of life,
life is to test out one's own striking-power.

The Self becomes more mature through suffering
until the Self rends the veils that cover God.
The God-seeing man sees himself only through God;
crying 'One God', he quivers in his own blood.
To quiver in blood is a great honour for love,
saw, stave and halter—these are love's festival.
Upon the road of love, whatever betides is good;
then welcome to the unlovingkindnesses of the Beloved!

Not my eye only desired the manifestation of God;
it is a sin to behold beauty without a company.
What is solitude? Pain, burning and yearning;
company is vision, solitude is a search.
Love in solitude is colloquy with God;
when love marches forth in display, that is to be a king!
Solitude and manifestation are the perfection of ardour,
both alike are states and stations of indigence.
What is the former? To desert cloister and church;
what is the latter? Not to walk alone in Paradise!
Though God dwells in solitude and manifestation,
solitude is the beginning, manifestation the end.
You have said that prophecy is a vexation:
when love becomes perfect, it fashions men.
It is delightful to go on God's road by caravan,
it is delightful to go in the world free as the soul.

TASIN OF CHRIST

Vision of the sage Tolstoy

In the midst of the mountain-range of Seven Deaths
is a valley where no bird stirs, no branches, no leaf;
the smoke encircling it turns the moon's light to pitch,
the sun in its broad heavens seems dying of thirst.
A river of quicksilver flows through that valley
meandering like the stream of the Milky Way.
Before it the hollows and heights of the road are nothing,
so swift its current, wave on wave, twist on twist.

A man stood, drowned up to his waist, in that quicksilver
uttering a thousand ineffectual laments.
Rain, wind and water were not his portion—
athirst he, and no water save the quicksilver.
On the bank I espied a slim-bodied woman
whose eyes would have waylaid a hundred caravans,
one that taught infidelity to the Church-elders,
her glance turned ugly to beautiful, beautiful to ugly.
I said to her, 'Who are you? What is your name?
What is this utter lamentation and weeping?'
She said, 'In my eye is the spell of the Samiri;
my name is Ifrangin, my profession is wizardry.'
All of a sudden that silvery stream froze,
the bones of that youth broke in his body.
He cried aloud, 'Alas, alas for my destiny!
Alas for my ineffectual lamentation!'
Ifrangin said, 'If you have eyes to see,
look a little also at your own deeds.
The Son of Mary, that Lamp of all creation
whose light lit up the world dimensioned and
undimensioned—
that Pilate, and that cross, that pallid face—
what wrought you, what wrought he beneath the skies!
You, to whose soul the joy of faith is forbidden,
worshipper of idols fashioned of raw silver,
you did not know the worth of the Holy Spirit,
you bought the body, gambled away the soul!'

The reproach of that fair woman, drunken with blandish-
ment,
was a lancet that pierced the youth's heart.
He said, 'You who display wheat and sell barley,
because of you Shaikh and Brahmin sell their own country.
Your infidelities have debased reason and religion,
your profit-mongerings have cheapened love.
Your love is torment, and secret torment at that;
your hatred is death, and sudden death at that!
You have associated with water and clay,

you have stolen away God's servant from Him.
Wisdom, which loosened the knots of things,
to you has given only thoughts of devastation.
That man whose substance is true knows well
your crime is heavier than my crime.
His breath restored the departed soul to the body;
you make the body a mausoleum for the soul.
What we have done unto His humanity
His community has done unto His divinity.
Your death is life for the people of the world:
wait now, and see what your end shall be!'

TASIN OF MOHAMMED

The Spirit of Abū Jahl Laments in the Sanctuary of the Kaaba

My breast is riven and anguished by this Mohammed;
his breath has put out the burning lamp of the Kaaba.
He has sung of the destruction of Caesar and Chosroes,
he has stolen away from us our young men.
He is a wizard, and wizardry is in his speech:
these two words 'One God' are very unbelief.
So he has rolled up the carpet of our fathers' faith
and has done with our Lord Gods what he has done.
The blow of his fist has scattered Lat and Manat:
take vengeance upon him, you created beings!
He bound his heart to the invisible, broke with the visible,
his incantation shattered the living, present image.
It is wrong to attach the eye to the invisible;
that which comes not into sight—wherever is it?
It is blindness to make prostration to the invisible;
the new religion is blindness, and blindness is remoteness.
To bend double before an undimensioned God—
such prayers bring no joy to the worshipper.

His creed cuts through the rulership and lineage
of Koraish, denies the supremacy of the Arabs;
in his eyes lofty and lowly are the same thing—

he has sat down at the same table with his slave.
He has not recognized the worth of the noble Arabs
but associated with uncouth Abyssinians;
redskins have been confounded with blackskins,
the honour of tribe and family has been destroyed.
This equality and fraternity are foreign things—
I know very well that Salman is a Mazdakite;
The son of Abdullah has been duped by him
and he has brought disaster upon the Arab people.
Hashim's progeny have become estranged one from another,
a couple of prayers have utterly blinded them.
What is alien stock, compared with the Adnani,
what betokens Sahbani speech to the barbarian?
The eyes of the elect of the Arabs have been darkened;
will you not rise up, Zuhair, from the dust of the tomb?
You who are for us a guide through this desert,
shatter the spell of the chant of Gabriel!

Tell again, you Black Stone, now tell again,
tell again what we have suffered through Mohammed!
Hubal, thou who acceptest the excuses of thy servants,
seize back thy temple from the irreligious ones;
expose their flock unto the ravening wolves,
make their dates bitter upon the palm-tree!
Let loose a burning wind on the air of the desert
as if they were stumps of fallen-down palm-trees.
O Manat, O Lat, go not forth from this abode,
or if you leave this abode, go not from our hearts!
You who have forever a lodging in our eyes,
tarry a little, *if you intend to depart from me.*

THE SPHERE OF MERCURY

Visitation to the Spirits of Jamal al-Din Afghani and Sa'id Halim Pasha

A handful of dust so carried forward its task
to the contemplation of its own manifestations:
either I fell into the net of being and existence
or existence became a prisoner in my net!
Have I made a chink in yon azure curtains?
Am I of the skies, or are the skies of me?
Either heaven has taken my heart into its breast
or it is my heart that has seized heaven.
Is this external then internal? What is it?
What manner of thing is it the eye sees? What is it?
I beat my wings towards another heaven,
I see another world rising before me,
a world of mountains and plains, seas and dry land,
a world far more ancient than our earth,
a world grown out of a little cloud
that has never known the conquest of man—
images as yet unlimned on the tablet of existence
where no critic of nature has yet been born.

I said to Rumi, 'This wasteland is very fair,
very fair the tumult of the waters in the mountains.
I find no sign here of any living thing,
so whence comes the sound of the call to prayer?'
Rumi said, 'This is the station of the saints,
this heap of earth is familiar with our dust.
When the father of mankind departed out of Eden
he dwelt in this world for one or two days;
these expanses have felt the burning of his sighs,

heard his lamentations in the hour of dawn.
The visitors to this honourable station
are themselves pious men of lofty stations,
pious men such as Fudail and Bu Sa'id,
true gnostics like Junaid and Ba Yazid.
Rise up now, and let us pray together,
devote a moment or two to burning and melting.'

I went on, and saw two men engaged in prayer,
the acolyte a Turk, the leader an Afghan.
The Sage of Rum, in rapture continually,
his face radiant with an ecstasy of joy,
said, 'The East never gave birth to two better sons—
the plucking of their nails unravelled our knots:
Maulana Jamal, Sayyid of all Sayyids,
whose eloquence gave life to stone and sherd,
and passionate Halim, commander of the Turks
whose thoughts matched the loftiness of his station.
To offer prayer with such men is true devotion,
a labour else whose hoped-for wage is Paradise.

The recitation of that vigorous elder,
the Chapter of the Star in that silent plain—
a recital that to move Abraham to ecstasy,
to enrapture the pure spirit of Gabriel;
the heedful heart becomes restless in the breast,
the cry 'No god but God' rises from the tombs;
it imparts to smoke the quivering of the flame,
bestows on David ardour and intoxication;
at his recital every mystery was revealed,
the Heavenly Archetype appeared unveiled.

After prayer I rose up from my place
and kissed his hand in all humility.

Rumi said, 'A mote that travels the skies,
in its heart a whole world of fire and passion!
Only upon himself he has opened his eyes,
yielded his heart to no man, is utterly free;
swiftly he paces through the expanse of Being—
jestingly, I call him Zinda-Rud.'

Afghani

Zinda-Rud, tell us of our terrestrial world,
speak to us of our earth and sky.
A thing of dust, you are clear-eyed as the Holy Ones—
give us some tidings of the Mussulmans!

Zinda-Rud

In the heart of a people that once shattered the world
I have seen a conflict between religion and country.
The spirit is dead in the body through weakness of faith,
despairs of the strength of the manifest religion;
Turk, Persian, Arab intoxicated with Europe
and in the throat of each the fish-hook of Europe;
and East wasted by the West's imperialism,
Communism taken the lustre from religion and community.

Afghani

Religion and Country

The Lord of the West, cunning from head to toe,
taught the people of religion the concept of Country.
He thinks of the centre, while you are at discord—
give up this talk of Syria, Palestine, Iraq!
If you can discriminate between good and evil
you will not bind your hearts to clods, stones, bricks.
What is religion? To rise up from the face of the dust
so that the pure soul may become aware of itself!

He who has said 'God is He' is not contained
within the confines of this dimensioned order.
A grass-blade is of the earth, and yet rises from the earth;
alas, if the pure soul should die in the dust!
Although man sprang out of water and clay,
from water and clay rose-like drew colour and sap,
alas, if he wanders forever in water and clay,
alas, if he soars not higher than this station!
The body says, 'Go into the dust of the roadway';
the soul says, 'Look upon the expanse of the world!'
Man of reason, the soul is not contained in dimensions;
the free man is a stranger to every fetter and chain,
the free man rails against the dark earth
for it beseems not the falcon to act like a mouse.

This handful of earth to which you give the name
'country',
this so-called Egypt, and Iran, and Yemen—
there is a relationship between a country and its people
in that it is out of its soil that a nation rises;
but if you look carefully at this relationship
you will descry a subtlety finer than a hair.
Though it is out of the East that the sun rises
showing itself bold and bright, without a veil,
only then it burns and blazes with inward fire
when it escapes from the shackles of East and West;
drunk with splendour it springs up out of its East
that it may subject all horizons to its mastery;
its nature is innocent of both East and West,
though relationship-wise, true, it is an Easterner.

Communism and Capitalism

The author of *Das Kapital* came of the stock of Abraham,
that is to say, that prophet who knew not Gabriel;
since truth was implicit even within his error
his heart believed, though his brain was an infidel.

The Westerners have lost the vision of heaven,
they go hunting for the pure spirit in the belly.
The pure soul takes not colour and scent from the body,
and Communism has nothing to do save with the body.
The religion of that prophet who knew not truth
is founded upon equality of the belly;
the abode of fraternity being in the heart,
its roots are in the heart, not in water and clay.

Capitalism too is a fattening of the body,
its unenlightened bosom houses no heart;
like the bee that pastures upon the flower
it overpasses the petal, and carries off the honey,
yet stalk and leaf, colour and scent all make up the rose
for whose selfsame beauty the nightingale laments.
Surpass the talisman, the scent and colour,
bid farewell to the form, gaze only upon the meaning.
Though it is difficult to descry the inward death,
call not that a rose which in truth is clay.

The soul of both is impatient and intolerant,
both of them know not God, and deceive mankind.
One lives by production, the other by taxation
and man is a glass caught between these two stones.
The one puts to rout science, religion, art,
the other robs body of soul, the hand of bread.
I have perceived both drowned in water and clay,
both bodily burnished, but utterly dark of heart.
Life means a passionate burning, an urge to make,
to cast in the dead clay of the seed of a heart!

Sa'id Halim Pasha

East and West

For Westerners intelligence is the stuff of life,
for Easterners love is the mystery of all being.

Only through love intelligence gets to know God,
love's labours find firm grounding in intelligence;
when love is companioned by intelligence
it has the power to design another world.
Then rise and draw the design of a new world,
mingle together love with intelligence.
The flame of the Europeans is damped down,
their eyes are perceptive, but their hearts are dead;
they have been sore smitten by their own swords,
hunted down and slaughtered, themselves the hunters.
Look not for fire and intoxication in their vine;
not into their heavens shall rise a new age.
It is from your fire that the glow of life comes,
and it is your task to create the new world.

Mustafa Kemal, who sang of a great renewal,
said the old image must be cleansed and polished;
yet the vitality of the Kaaba cannot be made new
if a new Lat and Manat from Europe enter its shrine.
No, the Turks have no new melody in their lute,
what they call new is only the old tune of Europe;
no fresh breath has entered into their breast,
no design of a new world is in their mind.
Turkey perforce goes along with the existing world,
melted like wax in the flame of the world we know.
Originality is at the roots of all creation,
never by imitation shall life be reformed;
The living heart, creator of ages and epochs,
that soul is little enamoured of imitation:
if you possess the spirit of a true Mussulman
examine your own conscience, and the Koran—
a hundred new worlds lie within its verses,
whole centuries are involved in its moments;
one world of it suffices for the present age—
seize it, if the heart in your breast grasps truth.
A believing servant himself is a sign of God,
every world to his breast is as a garment;
and when one world grows old upon his bosom,
The Koran gives him another world!

Zinda-Rud

The barque of us terrestrials has no helmsman,
no one knows where the Koran's world lies.

Afghani

It is a world lost now in our breast,
a world awaiting yet the command 'Arise!'
A world without distinction of race and colour,
its evening is brighter than Europe's dawn;
a world cleansed of monarchs and of slaves,
a world unbounded, like the believer's heart,
a world so fair, that the effluence of one glance
planted the seed of it in Omar's soul.
Eternal it is, the impact of it ever new,
ever new the leaf and fruit of its sure foundations;
inwardly it is anxious not of change,
outwardly, every moment is revolution.
Behold, that world lies within your own heart;
now I will tell you of its firm foundations.

The Foundations of the Koranic World

1. *Man, God's Vicegerent*

In both worlds, everywhere are the marks of love;
man himself is a mystery of love.
Love's secret belongs not to the world of wombs,
not to Shem or Ham, Greece or Syria:
a star without East and West, a star unsetting
in whose orbit is neither North nor South.
The words *I am setting* tell his destiny,
their exegesis reaches from earth to heaven.
Death, grave, uprising, judgment are his estates,
the light and fire of the other world are his works;
himself is Imam, prayer and sanctuary,
himself the Ink, himself the Book and the Pen.
Little by little what is hidden in him becomes visible;

it has no boundaries, its kingdom no frontiers.
His being gives value to contingent things,
his equilibrium is the touchstone of contingent things.
What shall I declare of his sea without a shore?
All ages and all times are drowned in his heart.
That which is contained within man is the world,
that which is not contained within the world is man.
Sun and moon are manifest through his self-display;
even Gabriel cannot penetrate his privacy.
Loftier than the heavens is the station of man,
and the beginning of education is respect for man.

Man alive in heart, do you know what thing life is?
One-seeing love that is contemplating duality:
man and woman are bound one to the other,
they are the fashioners of the creatures of desire.
Woman is the guardian of the fire of life,
her nature is the tablet of life's mysteries;
she strikes our fire against her own soul
and it is her substance that makes of the dust a man.
In her heart lurk life's potentialities,
from her glow and flame life derives stability;
she is a fire from which the sparks break forth,
body and soul, lacking her glow, cannot take shape.
What worth we possess derives from her values
for we are all images of her fashioning;
if God has bestowed on you a glance aflame
cleanse yourself, and behold her sanctity.

You from whose faith the present age has taken all fire,
now I will tell you openly the secrets of the veil.
The joy of creation is a fire in the body
and society is lightened by that light,
and whosoever takes any portion of that fire
watches jealously over his private passion;
all the time he fixes his gaze on his own image

lest his tablet should receive any other image.
Mohammed chose solitude upon Mount Hira
and for a space saw no other beside himself;
our image was then poured into his heart
and out of his solitude a nation arose.
Though you may be an unbeliever in God,
yet you cannot gainsay the Prophet's glory.
Though you possess a soul illumined as Moses,
yet without solitude your thoughts remain barren;
by isolation the imagination becomes more vivid,
more vivid, more questing, more finding.
Science and passion are both stations of life
both take a share of the impact of events.
Science derives pleasure from verification,
love derives pleasure from creativeness.
Display is very precious to the verifier,
to the creator solitude is very precious.
The eye of Moses desired to behold Being—
that was all part of the pleasure of verification;
thou shalt not see Me contains many subtleties—
lose yourself a little while in this sea profound.
On all sides life's traces appear unveiled,
its fountain wells up in the heart of creation.
Consider the tumult that rages through all horizons;
inflict not on the Creator the trouble of display—
solitude is the protection of every artist,
solitude is the bezel in the artist's ring.

2. *Divine Government*

The servant of God has no need of any station,
no man is his slave, and he is the slave of none;
the servant of God is a free man, that is all,
his kingdom and laws are given by God alone,
his customs, his way, his faith, his laws are of God,
of God his foul and fair, his bitter and sweet.
The self-seeking mind heeds not another's welfare,
sees only its own benefit, not another's;
God's revelation sees the benefit of all,

its regard is for the welfare and profit of all.
Just alike in peace and in the ranks of war,
His joining and parting are without fear and favour;
when other than God determines the aye and nay
then the strong man tyrannises over the weak;
in this world command is rooted in naked power;
mastery drawn from other than God is pure unbelief.

The tyrannical ruler who is well-versed in power
builds about himself a fortress made up of edicts;
white falcon, sharp of claw and swift to seize,
he takes for his counsellor the silly sparrow
giving to tyranny its constitution and laws,
a sightless man giving collyrium to the blind.
What results from the laws and constitutions of kings?
Fat lords of the manor, peasants lean as spindles!

Woe to the constitution of the democracy of Europe!
The sound of that trumpet renders the dead still deader;
those tricksters, treacherous as the revolving spheres,
have played the nations by their own rules, and swept the board!
Robbers they, this one wealthy, that one a toiler,
all the time lurking in ambush one for another;
now is the hour to disclose the secret of those charmers—
we are the merchandise, and they take all the profits.
Their eyes are hard out of the love of silver and gold,
their sons are a burden upon their mothers' backs.
Woe to a people who, out of fear for the fruit,
carries off the very sap from the tree's trunk
and, that the plectrum wins no melody from its strings,
slays the infant yet unborn in its mother's womb.
For all its repertory of varied charms
I will take nothing from Europe except—a warning!
You enchained to the imitation of Europe, be free,
clutch the skirt of the Koran, and be free!

3. *The Earth is the Lord's*

The history of man throughout East and West
is a tale of wars, battles, revolts, for 'land';
one bride there is, and we are all her husbands,
that enchantress is without all and with all withal.
Her blandishments are nothing but guile and trickery,
she belongs neither to you nor to me either.
These stones and rocks have nothing in common with you;
they are the stuff of stillness, you are on a journey.
How can the sleeper and the wakeful mix together?
What has the planet to do with the fixed star?
God has called the earth simply our 'enjoyment',
this valueless 'enjoyment' is gratis, gratis.
You landowner, take a wise hint from me:
take from the land your food and grave, but take it not.
How long will its company last? You are, it is not;
you are a living being, it is a lifeless show.
You are an eagle, therefore get you about the skies,
open your wings and pinions, rise clear of the earth.
'The Earth is the Lord's': the inward meaning is plain,
and he who sees not this plain is an infidel.

I do not say, desert utterly dwelling and lane;
this world of colour and scent is your empery—
grain by grain gather the jewels from its soil,
falcon-like seize your prey out of its skies,
smite your axe against its mountain-ranges,
take light from your self and set it all afire.
Have nothing to do with the ancient ways of Azar
but hew out a new world to your own desire!
Yield not your heart to colour and scent, dwelling and lane;
the heart is His sanctuary, yield it only to Him.
Death without substance, without tomb and winding-sheet
is to lose oneself in riches, children, wife;
but he who has the words 'One God' by heart
can lose within himself a world entire.
What is the poverty of hunger, dancing, nakedness?
Poverty is true kingship; what is monkery?

4. *Wisdom is a Great Good*

God has declared, *Wisdom is a great good*;
wherever you may see this good, seize it.
Science gives pinions to words and sounds,
bestows purest substance on things without substance;
science finds a way even to heaven's zenith
to pluck the sight out of the sun's own eye.
Its transcript is the commentary of the cosmos,
the fate of the cosmos hangs upon its determining;
it says to the desert, 'Bubble up!' and it bubbles,
to the sea, 'Produce a mirage!' and it produces it.
Its eye beholds all the events in creation
that it may see the sure foundations of creation;
if it attaches its heart to God, it is prophecy,
but if it is a stranger to God, it is unbelief.
Science without the heart's glow is pure evil,
for then its light is darkness over sea and land,
its rouge renders the whole world black and blind,
its springtide scatters the leaves of all being,
sea, plain and mountain, quiet garden and villa
are ravaged by the bombs of its aeroplanes.
It is its fire that burns the heart of Europe,
from it springs the joy of raiding and robbing;
it turns topsy-turvy the course of the days,
despoils the peoples of their capital.
Its power becomes the faithful ally of Satan;
light becomes fire by association with fire.
To slay Satan is indeed a difficult task,
since he is hidden within the depths of the heart;
better is it to make him a true Mussulman,
better to smite him dead with the sword of the Koran.
God save us from majesty that is without beauty,
God save us from separation without union!
Science without love is a demonic thing,
science together with love is a thing divine;
science and wisdom without love are a corpse,
reason is an arrow that never pierced the target.
With the vision of God make the blind to see,
convert Abu Lahab into an impetuous Haidar!

Zinda-Rud

You have displayed the foundations of the Book of God,
yet is yonder world still veiled in a shroud.
Why does it not strip off the veil from its face,
why does it not issue yet out of our hearts?
Before us lies a whole world wasting away,
a nation quietly reposing in its own dust;
the heart's ardour of Tartar and Kurd is vanished—
either the Mussulmans are dead, or the Koran is dead.

Sa'id Halim Pasha

The religion of God is more shameful than unbelief,
because the mullah is a believer trading in unfaith;
in our eyes this dew-drop of ours is an ocean,
to his eyes our ocean is a dew-drop.
At the elegant graces of that Koran-vendor
I have seen the Trusty Spirit himself cry out!
His heart is a stranger to what lies beyond the sky,
for him the Archetype of the Book is but a fable;
having no share of the wisdom of the Prophet's religion,
his heaven is dark, being without any star.
Short of vision, blind of taste, an idle gossip,
his hairsplitting arguments have fragmented the Community.
Seminary and mullah, before the secrets of the Book,
are as one blind from birth before the light of the sun.
The infidel's religion is the plotting and planning of Holy War;
the mullah's religion is corruption in the Way of God.
The man of God is the soul of this dimensionate world;
say from me to him, who has gone into solitude,
'You whose thoughts are life itself to the believer,
whose breaths are confirmation to the Community,
having the sublime Koran by heart is your rite,
your religion the publishing of the Word of God.
You with whom God speaks, how long will you hang your head?

Come, bring forth your hand out of your sleeve!
Speak of the history of the 'white' people,
speak to the gazelle of the vastness of the desert.
Your nature is illumined by the Chosen One,
so declare now, where is our station?

The man of God takes not colour and scent from anyone,
the man of God receives colour and scent from God;
every moment there is in his body a fresh soul,
every moment he has, like God, a new labour.
Declare the secrets to the believer,
declare the exposition of the mystery of *Every day*.
The caravan has no halting-place but the Sanctuary,
the caravan has naught but God in its heart;
I do not say that its road is different—
it is the caravan that is different, different its regard.

Afghani

Have you any acquaintance with the Traditions of the Chosen One?
'God's religion came a stranger into the world.'
I will tell you the meaning of this virgin saying.
The 'strangerhood' of religion is not the poverty of God's remembrancers;
for the man who is truly a researcher
'strangerhood' of religion refers to the scarceness of its verses.
The 'strangerhood' of religion every time is of a different kind;
ponder well this subtelty, if you have eyes to see.
Fasten your heart again to the perspicuous Verses
that you may seize a new age in your lasso.
No man knows the inner secrets of the Book;
Easterners and Westerners alike twist and turn this way and that.
The Russians have laid down a new design;

they have taken bread and water, and jettisoned religion.
Behold truth, speak truth, seek only truth;
speak one or two words from me to the people.

Afghani's Message to the Russian People

One thing is the goal and aim of the Koran,
other the rite and ritual of the Moslem;
in his heart there is no burning fire,
the Chosen One is not living in his breast.
The believer has not eaten the fruit of the Koran,
in his cup I have seen neither wine nor beer.
He broke the magic spell of Caesar and Chosroes
and himself sat on the throne of empire;
when the young shoot of power gathered strength,
his religion took on the shape of empire.
But empire changes the gaze entirely,
reason, understanding, usage and way alike.

You who have laid down a new plan,
and disengaged your heart from the ancient system,
like us Moslems you have broken
the bone of imperial rule in this world.
So that you may light a lamp in your heart
take a warning from our past history;
set your foot firm in the battle,
circle no more about this Lat and Hubal.
This aged world requires a nation
that shall be both bearer of good tidings and warner.
Return again to the peoples of the East;
your 'days' are bound up with the 'days' of the East.
You have kindled a new flame in the soul,
your heart houses a new night and day.
The rite and religion of the Franks have grown old;
look no more towards that ancient cloister.
You have finished now with lords;
pass on from 'no', march onwards to 'but'—

pass on from 'no', if you are a true seeker,
that you may take the road of living affirmation.
You who desire a new world-order,
have you sought for it a firm foundation?

You have expunged the ancient tale chapter by chapter;
illumine your thoughts from the Archetype of the Book.
Who gave the black man the White Hand?
Who gave the good news of no Caesar, no Chosroes?
Transcend the many-coloured splendours,
find yourself by abandoning Europe!
If you are apprised by the Westerners' cunning
give up the wolf, take on the lion's trade.
What is wolfishness? The search for food and means;
the Lion of the Lord seeks freedom and death.
Without the Koran, the lion is a wolf;
the poverty of the Koran is the root of empire.
The poverty of the Koran is the mingling of meditation
    and reason—
I have never seen reason perfect without meditation.
Meditation? To school pleasure and passion;
this is the affair of the soul, not the affair of lip and palate.
From it arise the flames that burn the breast,
it does not accord with your temperament yet.
Martyr of the delicate beauty of reason,
I will tell you of the revelations of reason!

What is the Koran? Sentence of death for the master-man,
succour for the slave without food and destitute.
Look not for good from the money-grubbing manikin—
You will not attain piety, until you expend.
What pray is born of usury? Tumults!
No one knows the pleasure of 'a good loan'.
Usury darkens the soul, hardens the heart like a stone,
makes man a ravening beast, without fangs and claws.
It is lawful to draw one's sustenance from the soil—

this is man's 'enjoyment', the property of God.
The believer is the trustee, God is the possessor;
whatever you see other than God is perishing.
God's banner has been beaten down by kings,
their entry has reduced townships to misery.
Our bread and water are of one table;
the progeny of Adam are *as a single soul.*
When the Koran's design descended into this world
it shattered the images of priest and pope;
I speak openly what is hidden in my heart—
this is not a book, it is something other!
When it has entered the soul, the soul is transformed;
when the soul has been transformed, the world is changed.
Like God, it is at once hidden and manifest,
living and enduring, yes, and speaking.
In it are the destinies of East and West—
realise then the lightning-like swiftness of thought!
It told the Moslem, 'Put your life in your hands;
give whatever you possess beyond your needs.'
You have created a new law and order;
consider it a little in the light of the Koran
and you will understand life's heights and depths,
you will comprehend the destiny of life.

Our assembly is without wine and cupbearer,
yet the melodies of the Koran's instrument are immortal;
if our plectrum now strikes without effect,
Heaven houses thousands of excellent strummers.
God's remembrance requires not nations,
it transcends the bounds of time and space.
God's remembrance is apart from the remembrance of every remembrancer—
what need has it of Greek or Syrian?
If God should remove it from us
He can if He will transfer it to another people.
I have seen the blind conformity and opinionatedness of Moslems
and every moment my soul trembles in my body;

I fear for the day when it shall be denied to them.
and its fire shall be kindled in quite other hearts.

The Sage of Rum bids Zinda-Rud intone a song

The Sage of Rum, that man filled wholly with ecstasy and passion,
I know what effect these words had on his soul;
he drew from his breast a heart-rending sigh,
his tears ran redder than the blood of martyrs.
He, whose arrows pierced only the hearts of heroes,
turned his gaze upon Afghani, and spoke:
'The heart must throb with blood like the twilight,
the hand must be thrust into the saddle-straps of God;
hope moves the soul to flow like a running river,
the abandonment of hope is eternal death.'
He looked at me again, and said: 'O Zinda-Rud,
with a couplet set all being afire.
Our camel is weary and the load is heavy;
more bitter must be the song of the caravaneer.
The proving of holy men is through adversity,
it is right to make the thirsty yet more athirst.
Like Moses depart from the River Nile,
stride out like Abraham towards the fire.
A melody of one who catches the scent of the Beloved
bears a people onwards even to the Beloved's street.

The Song of Zinda-Rud

You say that these roses and tulips are permanent here;
no, they are travellers all, like the waves of the breeze.
Where is the new truth which we seek, and do not find?
Mosque, school and tavern, all alike are barren.
Learn a word from your own self, and in that word burn,
for in this convent all lack Moses' fire.
Speak not of the striving for purity of these monastery-dwellers,

they are all dishevelled of hair, blankets unwashed.
What temples they have fashioned within the Sanctuary,
these unitarians of one thought, but all split in two!
The problem is not that the hour of feasting has passed,
the problem is that they are all without sweetmeats and boon-companion!

THE SPHERE OF VENUS

Between us and the light of the sun there hang
how many veils of space fold upon fold!
A hundred curtains have been suspended before us,
intertwisted firework displays,
that the unardent heart may increase in ardour
and become agreeable to branch, leaf and fruit.
Through its glow blood leaps in the tulip's veins,
its dance transmutes the stream to quicksilver.
Even so the pure spirit rises from the dust,
the pure spirit flees towards whither towards is not;
on that road are but death and resurrection, resurrection and death,
no other provision save fever and glowing.
Into that expanse of a hundred azure heavens
plunging continually, it surges out anew;
itself its own sanctuary, its own Abraham,
self-offering, like him who was sacrificed to God.
Before it the nine heavens are nine Khaibars,
its smiling is of the stature of Haidar.
It is this incessant conflict that purifies the spirit,
makes it firm, speedy, nimble,
it spreads its wings in the broadness of light,
its talons seize Gabriel and the houris,
that it may take its share in *the eye swerved out*
and stand guardian in the ranks of God's servants.

I do not know where my own station is,
I only know that it is apart from all friends.
Deep within me rages a war without horsemen and armies;
he well descries it who has vision like me.
Men are ignorant of the conflict between unbelief and faith,
my soul is lonely, like Zain al-Abidin;

none is apprised of the station and the way,
but for my song there is no lamp to light the path.
Infant, youth, old man—all are drowned in the sea,
only one poor soul has won his way to the shore.
I have drawn aside the curtains of this tent;
I am fearful of union, and lament for separation.
If union be the end of yearning, beware;
how blessed the sighs and vain lamentations!
The wayfarer searches little for the high-road
if to be carefree is congenial to his soul.
My soul is such that, for the joy of gazing,
it every moment desires a new world.
Rumi, well aware of the states of my soul,
said: 'Do you desire another world? Take it!
Love is cunning, and we are counters in his hand;
look ahead—we are in the land of Venus.
This world too subsists on water and clay,
a sanctuary enveloped in purest musk,
with a glance that burns and rends all veils
pass within its clouds and mists
and you will see therein the ancient gods;
I know them all, one by one—
Baal, Marduk, Ya'uq, Nasr, Fasr,
Ramkhan, Lat, Manat, Asr, Ghasr;
every one of them offers proof of its immortality
in the temper of this age that knows no Abraham.'

The assembly of the gods of the ancient peoples

That tempestuous wind, those night black clouds—
in their darkness the lightning itself had lost its lustre;
an ocean suspended in their air,
its skirt rent, few pearls pouring,
its shore invisible, its waves high-surging,
high-surging, powerless to battle with the winds.
Rumi and I in that sea of pitch
were as phantoms in the bedchamber of the mind—
he much-travelled, I new to travel,
my eyes impatient to gaze abroad.

Continually I cried: 'My sight is inadequate,
I do not see where the other world may be!'
Presently a mountain-range appeared,
a river, a broad meadow appeared,
mountain and plain embracing a hundred springtides—
fragrant with musk came the breeze from the hills.
Songs of birds conspiring together,
fountains, and verdant herbs half-grown.
The body was fortified by the emanation of that air,
the pure spirit in the flesh keener of vision.
I fixed my gaze on the top of a mountain;
joyful the mountain, the slope, the stretching plain;
a lovely valley, even, not sinking nor rising—
the water of Khizr would have need of such a land.
In this valley were the ancient gods,
there the God of Egypt, here the Lord of Yemen,
there a Lord of the Arabs, here of Iraq,
this one the god of union, that the god of separation,
here an offspring of the sun, and the moon's son-in-law,
another looking to the consort of Jupiter,
one holding a two-edged sword in his hand,
another with a serpent wreathed about his throat.
Each one was trembling at the Beautiful Name,
each wounded by the smiting of Abraham.
Mardukh said: 'Man has fled from God,
fled from church and sanctuary, lamenting,
and to augment his vision and perception
turns his gaze backwards to the past age.
He takes delight in ancient relics,
makes speeches about our theophanies.
Time has revealed a new legend;
a favourable wind is wafting from younder earth.'
Baal in excess of joy chanted sweetly
unveiling our secrets to the gods.

Song of Baal

Man has rent younder azure veil
and, beyond the sky, has seen no God.

What is there in man's heart but thoughts
like waves, this upsurging and that fleeing?
His soul takes repose in the sensible;
would that the past age might return!
Long live the European orientalist
who has drawn us forth from the tomb!
Ancient gods, our time has come!

Behold, the ring of unity is broken,
Abraham's people have lost the joy of Alast;
its company is scattered, its cup in fragments,
the cup which was drunken with the wine of Gabriel.
Free man has fallen into the bonds of directions,
joined up with fatherland and parted from God;
his blood is cold of the glory of the ancients,
the Elder of the Sanctuary has tied the Magian girdle.
Ancient gods, our time has come!

The days of joy have returned to the world,
religion has been routed by sovereignty and lineage.
What thought is there now of the lamp of the Chosen One,
seeing that a hundred Bu Lahabs blow it out?
Though the cry 'There is no god' rises up still
how should that remain on the lips which has gone from the heart?
The West's enchantment has revived Ahriman;
the day of God is pale-cheeked, fearful of the night.
Ancient gods, our time has come!

Religion's chain must be loosed from his neck,
our slave was ever a free slave;
since the ritual prayers are heavy for him,
we seek only one prayer, and that without prostration.
Passions are elevated by songs,

so what pleasure is there in prayers without hymns?
Better the demon that makes itself visible
than a God to whom the Unseen is meet.
Ancient gods, our time has come!

We plunge into the Sea of Venus and behold the spirits of Pharaoh and Kitchener

The Sage of Rum, that master of fair Report
whose blow has the power of Abraham's fist,
chanted this song in the world of intoxication
and all the ancient gods prostrate fell.

Ghazal

Again one must gaze on the past and the future;
ho, rise up, for one must think anew.
Love carries its load on the she-camel of Time;
are you a lover? You must make your mount of evening and morn.
Our elder said, 'The world follows not a constant way,
one must close one's eyes to its joys and griefs.
If, having abandoned the world, you intend Him,
first you must pass away from your self.'
I said to him, 'In my heart are many Lats and Manats.'
He said, 'You must destroy this idol-house utterly.'

Again he said to me: 'Rise up, boy,
cling only to my skirt, boy.
Yonder mountains, yonder heights without a Moses,
so covered with snow as to seem a heap of silver,
beyond them stretches a diamond-shining ocean,
its depths even more translucent than its surface;
undisturbed by wave or torrent,
in its nature an eternal quiet.
This is the place of power-drunk arrogants
denying the Unseen, worshipping the seen;

that one from the East, the other from the West,
both at war and blows with the men of God.
One has had on his neck the staff of Moses,
the other struck asunder by a dervish's sword,
both Pharaohs, one little, the other great,
both dying of thirst in the embrace of the sea;
each is familiar with the bitterness of death—
the death of tyrants is one of God's signs.
Follow me closely and fear no one;
place your hand in mine and fear no one.
I will rend apart the sea like Moses;
I will guide you into its very breast.'

The sea opened to us its breast—
or was it air, that appeared as a water?
Its depths were a valley without colour and scent,
a valley whose darkness was fold on fold.
The Sage of Rum chanted the Sura of Taha;
under the sea streamed down moonshine.
Mountains washed, naked and cold,
and amid them two bewildered men
who first cast a glance on Rumi,
then gazed one upon the other.
Pharaoh cried, 'What wizardry! What a river of light!
whence comes this dawn, this light, this apparition?'

Rumi

All that is hidden through Him is manifest;
the origin of this Light is from the White Hand.

Pharaoh

Ah, I have gambled away the coin of reason and religion;
I saw, but did not recognize this light.
World-rulers, gaze all upon me;

world-destroyers, gaze all upon me!
Woe to a people blinded by avarice
who have robbed the tomb of rubies and pearls!
A human shape dwells in a museum
with a legend upon its silent lips
telling the history of imperialism
and giving visions to the blind.
What is the grand design of imperialism?
To seek security by contriving division.
From such evil doctrine the fate of rulership declines,
the contrivances of rulership become void and confused.
If I could only see God's interlocutor again
I would beg from him a heart aware.

Rumi

Government without spiritual light is raw, raw,
imperial power without the White Hand is a sin.
Rulership is strong through the weakness of the subjects,
its roots are firm through the deprivation of the deprived.
The crown derives from tribute and the yielding of tribute;
if a man be a rock, he soon becomes glass.
Armies, prisons, chains are banditry;
he is the true ruler who needs not such apparatus.

Kitchener of Khartoum

The goal of the people of Europe is lofty,
they excavate not any grave for rubies and pearls—
the history of Egypt, Pharaoh and Moses
can be seen from ancient monuments.
Science and wisdom is simply the unveiling of secrets;
wisdom without research is utterly worthless.

Pharaoh

Science and wisdom uncovered my tomb;
but what was there to find in the Mahdi's grave?

The Sudanese Dervish appears

A restless lightning flashed in the water,
waves surged and rolled in the water;
a sweet scent wafted from the rose-garden of Paradise,
the spirit of that dervish of Egypt appeared.
His fire melted the pearl in the oyster-shell,
melted the stone in the breast of Kitchener.
He cried, 'Kitchener, if you have eyes to see,
behold the avenging of a dervish's dust!
Heaven granted no grave for your dust,
gave no resting-place but the salty ocean.'
Then the words broke in his throat;
from his lips a heart-rending sigh was loosed.
'Spirit of the Arabs', he cried, 'arise;
like your forebears, be the creator of new ages!
Fouad, Feisal, Ibn Saoud,
how long will you twist like smoke on yourselves?
Revive in the breast that fire which has departed,
bring back to the world the day that has gone.
Soil of Batha, give birth to another Khalid,
chant once more the song of God's Unity.
In your plains taller grow the palm-trees;
shall not a new Farouk arise from you?
World of musky-hued believers,
from you the scent of eternal life is coming to me.
How long will you live without the joy of journeying,
how long with your destiny in alien hands?
How long will you desert your true station?
My bones lament in the deep like a reed-pipe;
are you afraid to suffer? The Chosen One declared,
"For man the day of suffering is the day of purification."

'Cameleer, our friends are in Yathrib, we in Nejd;
sing that song which will stir the camel to ecstasy.
The cloud has rained, grasses have sprouted from the earth,
it may be that the camel's pace grows languid.
My soul wails of the pain of separation;
take the road where fewer grasses grow.

My camel is drunk with the grass, I for the Beloved;
the camel is in your hands, I in the hands of the Beloved.
They have made a way for waters into the desert,
upon the mountains the palm fronds are washed.
Yonder two gazelles one after the other—
see how they are descending from the hill,
for a moment drink from the desert spring
and then glance upon the traveller.
The dew has softened the sands of the plain like silk,
the highway is not hard for the camel:
the clouds ring on ring like the wings of the partridge—
I fear the rain, for we are far from the goal.
Cameleer, our friends are in Yathrib, we in Nejd;
sing that song which will stir the camel to ecstasy.'

THE SPHERE OF MARS

The Martians

For an instant I closed my eyes in the waters,
for a little in the depths I broke away from myself,
bore my baggage towards another world,
with another time, another space.
Our sun reached its horizons,
creating a different kind of night and day.
The body is a stranger to the spirit's wont and way
which dwells in time, yet is a stranger to time.
Our soul accords with every fire there is,
its time rejoices in every day there is;
it grows not old with the flight of time,
the days illumine the world through its light.
The ceaseless revolution of day and night from it derives;
make it your journey, for the very world springs from it.

A broad meadow with a tall observatory
whose telescope lassoed the Pleiades—
is this the nine-domed retreat of Khizr,
or is it the dark territory of our earth?
Now I searched for the bounds of its immensity,
anon I gazed upon the expanse of heaven.
The Sage of Rum, that guide of the visionaries,
spoke: 'Behold, this world is Mars;
like our world, it is a talisman of colours and scents,
having cities and habitations, palaces and streets.
Its dwellers are skilled in many arts, like the Franks,
excelling us in physical and psychical sciences.
They have greater dominion over time and place
because they are cleverer at the science of space;
they have so penetrated into its essence
that they have seen its every twist and turn.

Earth's dwellers—their hearts are bound to water and clay;
in this world, body is in bondage to heart.
When a heart makes its lodging in water and clay,
with water and clay it makes what it wills;
intoxication, joy, happiness are at the disposal of the soul,
the soul determines the body's absence and presence.
In our world, existence is a duality,
soul and body, the one invisible, the other visible;
for terrestrials, soul and body are bird and cage,
whereas the thought of Martians is unitive.
When the day of separation arrives for any,
he becomes livelier from the flame of separation;
a day or two before the day of death
he proclaims his decease to his fellows.
Their soul is not nourished by the body,
therefore it has not become habituated to the body.
Death is to draw in the body,
death is to flee from the world into one's self.
This discourse is too high for your thought
because your soul is dominated by your body.
You must wander here for a moment or two;
God gives not such an opportunity to everyone.'

The Martian astronomer comes out of the observatory

An aged man, his beard white as snow,
having expended many years upon science and wisdom,
keen of eye like the Western sages,
his raiment like the robes of a Christian monk,
far on in years, yet tall of stature as a cypress,
his features glowing like a Turk of Merv,
well-versed in the wont and way of every road,
the deep thoughts evident in his eyes,
seeing a man approaching, he opened like a flower
and spoke in the tongue of Tusi and Khayyám.
'A form of clay, prisoner to Quantity and Quality,
has come forth from the abode of Under and Over,
given flight to earth without aid of aircraft,
lent to the fixed stars the essence of the planet!'

His speech and comprehension flowed like a river;
I was lost in stupefaction at his words:
is this all a dream, or a trick of magic?
Pure Persian proceeding from a Martian's lips!
He continued: 'In the time of the Chosen One
there was a Martian, a man pure of soul,
who opened his world-beholding eyes on your world
and set his heart on travelling the confines of man.
He spread his wings in the vast expanses of being
until he alighted in the desert of Hejaz.
He wrote down all that he saw in East and West,
his picture more colourful than the Garden of Paradise.
I too have been in Iran and Europe,
I have travelled in the realms of Nile and Ganges,
I have seen America and Japan and China,
investigating the metals of the earth.
I have knowledge of earth's nights and days,
I have journeyed through its lands and seas.
The tumults of Adam's sons are open before me,
though man is not intimate with our labours.'

Rumi

I am of the skies, my companion is of the earth,
intoxicated, yet he has not tasted the veins of the vine;
a man intrepid, his name is Zinda-Rud,
his drunkenness derived from contemplating existence.
We who have chanced thus upon your city
are in the world, yet free from the world.
In our quest for ever new apparitions
be our companion on the road for a little time.

The Martian Sage

These are the environs of Marghadin of Barkhiya—
Barkhiya is the name of our ancestor.
Farzmarz, the tempter to all evil,
came up to Barkhiya once in Paradise;
'How can you remain here content?' he cried.
'For many ages you have been dominated by God.

There is a world far better than your abode,
compared with which Paradise itself is but a moment's springtide;
that world is loftier than all other worlds,
that world is more sublime than spacelessness.
God Himself knows nothing of that world;
I have never seen a world more free.
God does not interfere in its ordering,
it has no Book, no Prophet, no Gabriel,
no circumambulations, no prostrations there,
no prayers, no thanksgivings.'
Barkhiya replied, 'Depart, you sorcerer,
pour your own image upon that world!'
Since our ancestor did not succumb to his guile
God entrusted to us another world.
So enter this God-given kingdom;
behold Marghadin and its laws and customs.

Tour of the city of Marghadin

Marghadin and those lofty edifices—
what can I say of that noble city?
Its inhabitants sweet of speech as honey,
comely their faces, gentle their manners, simple their apparel,
their thoughts innocent of the burning fever of gain,
they were intimate with the secrets of the sun's alchemy;
who so of them desires silver or gold gathers it from light,
even as we gather salt from the briny sea.
The aim of science and art there is service,
no one weighs work done against gold;
no one is even acquainted with dinars and dirhams,
these idols may not enter the sanctuary.
The demon of the machine has no power over nature,
the skies are not blackened by smoke;
the lamp of the hard-toiling farmer is always bright,
he is secure from the plundering of the landlords,
his tillage is not a struggle for water,
his harvest is his own, no other shares in it.

In that world there are no armies, no squadrons,
none gains his livelihood by killing and murder;
In Marghadin no pen wins lustre
from inscribing and disseminating lies;
in the market-places there is no clamour of the workless,
no whining of beggars afflicts the ear.

The Martian Sage

No one here is a mendicant or destitute,
slave and master, ruler and ruled, here are none.

Zinda-Rud

Mendicant and destitute are so by God's decree,
by God's decree ruler and ruled;
none but God is the creator of destiny
and against destiny human design is powerless.

The Martian Sage

If your heart bleeds on account of one destiny,
petition God to decree another destiny;
if you pray for a new destiny, that is lawful,
seeing that God's destinies are infinite.
Earthlings have gambled away the coin of selfhood,
not comprehending the subtle meaning of destiny;
its subtlety is contained in a single phrase—
'If you transform yourself, it too will be transformed.'
Be dust, and fate will give you the winds;
be a stone, and it will hurl you against glass.
Are you a dew-drop? Your destiny is to perish;
are you an ocean? Your destiny is to endure.

Every moment you are fashioning new Lats and Manats;
inconstant one, do you look for constancy from idols?

So long as your faith is to accord not with your self
the world of your thoughts is your prison;
toil without treasure—such is destiny;
treasure without toil—such is destiny!
If this is the foundation of faith, ignorant fellow,
then the needy will become still more in need.
Woe to that religion which lulls you to sleep
and still holds you in sleep profound!
Is this religion, or magic and enchantment?
Is this religion, or a grain of opium?

Do you know whence comes the penetrating nature,
whence came this houri into your tenement of clay?
Do you know whence comes the sages' power of thought,
whence the potency of prayer in God's interlocutors?
Do you know whence came this heart, and its visitations,
whence these arts, these miracles?
Do you have fire of speech? That comes not from you;
do you have flame of action? That comes not from you.
All this is an overflow of the springtime of nature,
nature which derives from nature's Creator.
What is life? A mine of gems;
you are the trustee, its owner is Another.
A radiant nature glorifies the man of God,
to serve all God's creatures, that is his aim.
Service belongs to the wont and way of prophethood;
to seek a reward for service is mere commerce.

Even so this wind, earth, cloud, field,
orchard, meadow, palace, street, stones, bricks—
you who say, 'Our property is of ourselves',
ignorant one, all this belongs to God.
If you regard God's earth as your own,
then what means the verse, *Work not corruption*?
Adam's sons have given their hearts to Iblis,
and from Iblis I have seen only corruption.

None should convert a trust to his own use;
blessed is he who renders God's property up to God.
You have carried off what does not belong to you;
my soul sorrows for so unworthy a deed.
If you own a thing, that is meet and right,
but if you do not, say yourself, how is that proper?
Return to God the property of God
so that you may loose the knot of your involvement;
for why is there poverty and want under heaven's arch?
Because you say what is the Lord's belongs to you.
The man who has not leaped forth from water and clay
has shattered his own glass with his own stone.
You who cannot tell goal from path,
the value of every thing is measured by the regard.
So long as the pearl is your property, it is a pearl,
otherwise it is a pebble, worth less than a farthing.
View the world otherwise, and it will become other,
this earth and heaven will be transformed.

The Martian damsel who claimed to be a prophetess

We passed by thousands of streets and mansions;
on the edge of the city was a broad square
and in that square a swarm of men and women,
amidst them a woman with the stature of a tall pomegranate-tree.
Her face was radiant, but without the light of the soul,
as if its meaning were too hard to express;
her speech lacked fire, her eyes lacked tears,
not intimate with the joy of desire:
her breast was void of the ardour of youth,
blind and unreceptive to images her mirror;
she knew nothing of love and the laws of love,
she was a sparrow spurned by the hawk of love.
That sage who knew all subtleties spoke to us:
'This damsel is not of the Martians;
simple and free of guile, without artifice,
Farzmarz kidnapped her from the Franks
and made her expert in the craft of prophethood,

then let her loose upon this world,
She declared, "I have come down from heaven;
my message is the final message of time."
She speaks of the status of man and woman,
she speaks more openly of the secrets of the body.
The destiny of life in this end of time
I will now recount in the language of earthlings.'

Admonition of the Martian Prophetess

Women! Mothers! Sisters!
How long shall we live like fond darlings?
To be a darling here is to be a victim,
to be a darling is to be dominated and deprived.
We idly comb out our tresses
and think of men as our prey;
but man is a hunter in the guise of a quarry
and circles about you to lasso you.
His swooning ardours are but cunning and deceit,
cunning and deceit his anguish and agony and yearning.
Though that infidel makes a shrine of you,
he causes you to suffer much anguish and grief.
To be his consort is a torment of life,
union with him is poison, separation from him sugar.
A twisting serpent he—flee from his coils,
do not pour his poisons into your blood.
Maternity pales the cheeks of mothers;
O happy, to be free and without husband!

The divine revelation comes to me continuously
augmenting the delight I have in faith.
The time has come when by a miracle of science
it is possible to see the foetus within the body;
from life's field you may gather a harvest
of sons and daughters exactly as you choose,
and if the foetus accords not with our desire
it is the essence of religion ruthlessly to slay it.

After this age other ages will come
wherein new secrets shall be revealed;
the foetus will take nourishment of another kind,
without the night of the womb it will find the day.
Finally that being utterly demonic will die
even as died the creatures of the ancient days.
Tulips without scar, with skirt unstained,
not in need of dew, will rise from the earth.
Of their own accord the secrets of life will emerge,
life's string will yield melodies without a plectrum.
Oyster dying of thirst under the sea,
do not accept the scatterings of April;
rise up and wage war with nature,
that by your battling the maiden may be freed.
Woman's unitarianism is to escape from the union of two bodies;
be guardian of yourself, and tangle not with men!

Rumi

Regard the creed of this new-fangled age,
regard the harvest of irreligious education.
Love is the law and ritual of life,
religion the root of education; religion is love.
Love externally is ardent, fiery,
inwardly it is the Light of the Lord of the Worlds.
From its inward fever and glow, science and art derive,
science and art spring from its ingenious madness;
religion does not mature without Love's schooling;
learn religion from the company of the Lords of Love.

THE SPHERE OF JUPITER

The noble spirits of Hallaj, Ghalib, and Qurrat al-Ain Tahira, who disdained to dwell in Paradise, preferring to wander for ever

Let me be a ransom for this demented heart
which every instant bestows on me another desert;
whenever I take up a lodging, it says, 'Rise up!'
The self-strong man reckons the sea as but a pool.
Seeing that the signs of God are infinite
where, traveller, can the high-road end?
The task of science is to see and consume,
the work of gnosis is to see and augment;
science weighs in the balance of technology,
gnosis weighs in the balance of intuition;
science holds in its hand water and earth,
gnosis holds in its hand the pure spirit;
science casts its gaze upon phenomena,
gnosis absorbs phenomena into itself.

In quest of continuous manifestations
I travel through the skies, lamenting like a reed;
all this is by the grace of a pure-born saint
whose ardour fell upon my soul.
The caravan of these two scanners of existence
presently halted by the shores of Jupiter,
that world, that earth not yet complete,
circling about it moons swift of pace;
the glass of its vine was still empty of wine,
desire as yet had not sprouted from its soil.
Midnight, a world half day in the moon's gleam,

the air thereof neither chill nor torrid.
As I lifted my gaze towards heaven
I saw a star closer to me;
the awful prospect robbed me of my senses—
near and far, late and soon became transformed.
I saw before me three pure spirits
the fire in whose breasts might melt the world.
They were clad in robes of tulip hue,
their faces gleamed with an inner glow;
in fever and fervour since the moment of Alast,
intoxicated with the wine of their own melodies.
Rumi said, 'Do not go out of yourself so,
be quickened by the breath of these songs of fire.
You have never seen intrepid passion; behold!
You have never seen the power of this wine; behold!
Ghalib and Hallaj and the Lady of Persia
have flung tumult into the soul of the sanctuary.
These songs bestow stability on the spirit,
their warmth springs from the inmost heart of creation.'

The Song of Hallaj

Seek from your own earth a fire as yet unseen,
another's apparition is unworthy of your demand.
I have so fastened on myself my gaze, that though the beauty of the Beloved
fills all the world, I am left no time to contemplate.
I would not give for Jamshid's realm that verse of Naziri:
'He who is yet unslain belongs not to our tribe.'
Though reason whose trade is wizardry mustered an army,
your heart will not be dismayed, for Love is not alone.
You know not the way and are uninformed of the stage;
what melody is there that is not in Sulaima's lute?
Tell a tale of the hunting and fettering of sharks:
do not say, 'Our skiff knows not the face of the sea.'
I am disciple of the zeal of that wayfarer who never set foot
on any high-road that ran over mountains, deserts and seas.
Be partner with the ring of wine-bibbing dissolutes;
beware of allegiance to a Master who is not a man of tumult.

The Song of Ghalib

Come, let us change the rule of heaven,
let us change fate by revolving a heavy measure of wine;
though the police-captain makes trouble, we will not worry,
and if the king himself sends a present, we will reject it.
Though Moses converse with us, we will not say a word;
though Abraham be our host, we will decline him.
Battling, the tribute-snatchers of the grove
we will turn away from our garden's gate with empty basket;
peacefully, the birds that flutter their wings at dawn
we will send back from the grove to their nests.
You and I are of Haidar, so no wonder would it be
if we turn back the sun towards the East.

The Song of Tahira

If ever confronting face to face my glance should alight on you
I will describe to you my sorrow for you in minutest detail.
That I may behold your cheek, like the zephyr I have visited
house by house, door by door, lane by lane, street by street.
Through separation from you my heart's blood is flowing from my eyes
river by river, sea by sea, fountain by fountain, stream by stream.
My sorrowful heart wove your love into the fabric of my soul
thread by thread, thrum by thrum, warp by warp, woof by woof.
Tahira repaired to her own heart, and saw none but you
page by page, fold by fold, veil by veil, curtain by curtain.

The ardour and passion of these anguished lovers
cast fresh commotions into my soul;

ancient problems reared their heads
and made assault upon my mind.
The ocean of my thought was wholly agitated;
its shore was devastated by the might of the tempest.
Rumi said, 'Do not lose any time,
you who desire the resolution of every knot;
for long you have been a prisoner in your own thoughts,
now pour this tumult out of your breast!'

Zinda-Rud propounds his problems to the great spirits

Why do you keep far from the station of believers?
That is, why are you exiled from Paradise?

Hallaj

The free man who knows good and evil,
his spirit cannot be contained in Paradise.
The mullah's Paradise is wine and houris and page boys,
the Paradise of free men is eternal voyaging;
the mullah's Paradise is eating and sleeping and singing,
the lover's Paradise is the contemplation of Being.
The mullah's Resurrection is the splitting of the tomb and
  the trumpet's blast,
tumult-arousing Love is itself the Dawn of Resurrection.
Science is founded upon fear and hope,
lovers are troubled by neither hope nor fear;
science is fearful of the grandeur of creation,
Love is immersed in the beauty of creation;
science gazes upon the past and the present,
love cries, 'Look upon what is coming!'
Science has made compact with the canon of constraint
and has no other resource but constraint and resignation;
Love is free and proud and intolerant
and boldly investigates the whole of Being.
Our love is a stranger to complaining
even though it weeps the tears of drunkenness.

Our constrained heart is not truly constrained,
our arrow is not shot by any houri's glance;
our fire augments out of separation,
separation is congenial to our soul.
Life without prickings is no true life;
one must live with a fire under one's feet.
Such living is the destiny of the self
and through this destiny the self is built up.
A mote through infinite yearning becomes the envy of the sun,
in its breast the nine spheres cannot be contained;
when yearning makes assault upon a world
it transforms momentary beings into immortals.

Zinda-Rud

The wheeling of destiny is death and life;
no man knows what the wheeling of destiny is.

Hallaj

Whoever possesses the apparatus of destiny,
Iblis and death tremble before his might.
Predestination is the religion of men of zeal,
predestination for heroes is the perfection of power.
Ripe souls become yet riper through constraint
which for raw men is the embrace of the tomb.
Khalid constrained turns a world upside down;
for us, constraint tears us up by the roots.
The business of true men is resignation and submission;
this garment does not suit the weaklings.
You who know the station of the Sage of Rum,
do you not know the words of the Sage of Rum?
'A fire-worshipper there was in the time of Ba Yazid;
a blessed Moslem said to him,
"Better were it if you accepted the Faith
so that salvation and the excellence would be yours."
The other said, "Disciple, if this be faith

that the Shaikh of the World Ba Yazid possesses,
I cannot endure its glowing heat
which is too great for the strivings of my soul." '
Our concern is only with hope and fear;
not every man has the zeal to surrender.
You who say, 'This was to be, and so happened,
all things were tethered to a divine decree, and so happened,'
you have little understood the meaning of destiny,
you have seen neither selfhood nor God.
The believer true thus petitions God:
'We accord with you, so accord with us.'
His resolution is the creator of God's determination
and on the day of battle his arrow is God's arrow.

Zinda-Rud

Men of short vision have stirred up commotions
and hung God's true servant on the gibbet.
The hidden things of Being are manifest to you;
declare then, what was your crime?

Hallaj

The sound of the Last Trump was in my breast;
I saw a people hastening to the tomb,
believers with the character and colour of infidels
who cried 'No god but God' and denied the Self.
'God's bidding' they called a vain image
because it was bound to water and clay.
I kindled in my self the fire of life
and spoke to the dead of the mysteries of life.
The whole world has been founded on Selfhood,
love therein has been compounded with violence;
Selfhood is everywhere visible, yet invisible,
our gaze cannot endure to look on Selfhood;
within its light many fires lurk hidden,
from its Sinai creation's epiphanies shine.

Every moment every heart in this ancient convent
discourses, albeit secretly, of the Self;
whoever has not taken his share of its fire
has died in the world, a stranger to himself.
India and Iran alike are privy to its light,
but few there are who also know its fire.
I have spoken of its light and its fire;
confidant of my secret, see now my crime.
What I have done you too have done; beware!
You have sought to resurrect the dead: beware!

Tahira

From the sin of a frenzied servant of God
new creatures come into being;
unbounded passion rends veils apart,
removes from the vision the old and stale,
and in the end meets its portion in rope and gallows
neither turns back living from the Beloved's street.
Behold Love's glory in city and fields,
lest you suppose it has passed away from the world;
it lies concealed in the breast of its own time—
how could it be contained in such a closet as this?

Zinda-Rud

You who have been given the agony of the eternal quest,
explain to me the meaning of a verse of yours:
The dove is a handful of ashes, the nightingale a network of colour—
O lamentation, what is the true sign of a broken heart?

Ghalib

The lament that rises out of a broken heart—
I have seen its effect different in every place;

the dove is consumed through its influence,
the nightingale daubed with colours as its result.
In it, death is in the embrace of life,
one moment here is life, there is death;
such a colour as glowed in Mani's abode,
such a colour as begets colourlessness.
You know not, this is the station of colour and scent;
the portion of every heart is according to its ululation.
Either enter colour, or pass into colourlessness,
that you may grasp a token of the broken heart.

Zinda-Rud

A hundred worlds are manifest in this azure expanse;
are there saints and prophets in every world?

Ghalib

Consider well this being and not-being;
continuously worlds are coming into existence.
Wherever the tumultuous clamour of a world arises,
there too is a *Mercy unto all beings*.

Zinda-Rud

Speak more plainly; my understanding flags.

Ghalib

It were a sin to speak of these things more plainly.

Zinda-Rud

Then is the conversation of adepts unprofitable?

Ghalib

It is difficult to give tongue to this subtlety.

Zinda-Rud

You are wholly afire with the glow of the quest,
yet how strange, you cannot master mere words!

Ghalib

'Creation', 'Predestination', 'Guidance' are the beginning;
a *Mercy unto all beings* is the end.

Zinda-Rud

I have not yet glimpsed the face of the meaning;
if you possess a fire, then burn me!

Ghalib

You who like me descry the secrets of poetry,
these words overstretch the string of poetry;
the poets have adorned the banquet of words,
but these Moses lack the White Hand.
What you demand of me is unbelief,
an unbelief transcending poetry.

Hallaj

Wherever you see a world of colour and scent
out of whose soil springs the plant of desire
is either already illumined by the light of the Chosen One
or is still seeking for the Chosen One.

Zinda-Rud

I ask of you—though to ask is a sin—
the secret of that essence whose name is the Chosen One;
is it a man, or an essence in being
such as but rarely comes into existence?

Hallaj

Before him the whole world bows prostrate,
before him who called himself His servant.
'His servant' surpasses your understanding
because he is man, and at the same time essence.
His essence is neither Arab nor non-Arab;
he is a man, yet more ancient than man.
'His servant' is the shaper of destinies,
in him are deserts and flourishing cultivations;
'His servant' both increases life and destroys it,
'His servant' is both glass and heavy stone.
'Servant' is one thing, 'His servant' is another;
we are all expectancy, he is the expectation.
'His servant' is time, and time is of 'His servant';
we all are colour, he is without colour and scent.
'His servant' had beginning, but has no end;
what have our morn and eve to do with 'His servant'?
No man knows the secret of 'His servant',
'His servant' is naught but the secret of 'save God'.
'Save God' is the sword whose edge is 'His servant';
do you want it plainer? Say, He is 'His servant'.
'His servant' is the how and why of creation,
'His servant' is the inward mystery of creation.
The true meaning of these two verses becomes not clear
until you behold from the station of *Thou threwest not*.
Zinda-Rud, have done now with speaking and listening,
become drowned in the ocean of being, Zinda-Rud.

Zinda-Rud

I know so little—what is this business of Love?
Is it the joy of beholding? Then what is beholding?

Hallaj

The meaning of beholding that Last of Time
is to make his rule binding on oneself.
Live in the world like the Apostle of men and jinn
that like him you may be accepted by men and jinn
Then behold yourself—that is the same as beholding him;
his Sunna is a secret of his secrets.

Zinda-Rud

What is the beholding of the God of the nine spheres,
of Him without whose command moon and sun do not revolve?

Hallaj

First, to implant on one's soul the image of God,
then next to implant it on the world;
when the soul's image is perfected in the world,
to behold the commons is to behold God.
Blessed is the man whose single sigh
causes the nine heavens to circle about his dwelling;
woe to the dervish who, having uttered a sigh,
then closes his lips and draws back his breath!
Such a one never made God's rule to run in the world;
he ate barley-bread, but never fought like Ali;
he sought a convent and fled from Khaibar,
he practised monkhood and never saw royal power.
Do you possess God's image? The world is your prey;
destiny shares the same reins as your design.
The present age seeks to war with you;
imprint God's image on this infidel's tablet!

Zinda-Rud

God's image has been implanted on the world;
I do not know how it has been implanted.

Hallaj

It has been implanted by force of love
or it has been implanted by force of violence;
because God is more manifest in love,
love is a better way than violence.

Zinda-Rud

Declare, master of the secrets of the East,
what difference is there between the ascetic and the lover?

Hallaj

The ascetic is a stranger in this present world,
the lover is a stranger in the world to come.

Zinda-Rud

The end of gnosis is not-being—
what, is life to repose in annihilation?

Hallaj

The intoxication of lovers comes from emptied cups;
not-being is to be ignorant of gnosis.
You who seek your goal in annihilation,
non-existence can never discover existence.

Zinda-Rud

He who counted himself better than Adam,
in his jar and cup remains neither wine nor lees;
our handful of dust is acquainted with the skies—
where is the fire of that destitute one?

Hallaj

Speak little of that Leader of those in separation,
throat athirst, and eternally a blood-filled cup.
We are ignorant, he knows being and not-being;
his infidelity revealed to us this mystery,
how that from falling comes the delight of rising,
from the pain of waning springs the joy of waxing.
Love is to burn in his fire;
without his fire, burning is no burning.
Because he is more ancient in love and service,
Adam is not privy to his secrets.
Tear off the skirt of blind conformity
that you may learn God's Unity from him.

Zinda-Rud

You who hold the clime of the soul under your royal signet,
keep company with me a moment more.

Hallaj

We do not tolerate confinement to one station,
we are wholly and singly a yearning to soar;
every instant our occupation is to see and to quiver,
our labour is to fly without feathers and wings.

Iblis, Leader of the People of Separation, appears

The company of the radiant of heart is for a breath or two,
that breath or two is the substance of being and not-being;
it made love more tumultuous, and then passed,
endowed reason with vision, and then passed.
I closed my eyes to hold it still within me,
to transport it from my eyes to my heart.
Suddenly I saw the world had become dark,

become dark from space even to spacelessness.
In that night a flame appeared
from the midst of which an old man leaped forth
wrapped in a cloak of antimony grey,
his body immersed in wreathing smoke.
Rumi said, 'The Leader of the People of Separation!
How all a-fire, and what a cup of blood!

Ancient, seldom smiling, of few words,
his eyes scanning the soul within the body,
drunkard and mullah, philosopher and Sufi,
in practice like a toiling ascetic,
his nature alien to the joy of union,
his asceticism the abandonment of eternal beauty;
since it was not easy to break away from beauty,
he made a beginning with spurning adoration.
Gaze a little at his visitations,
gaze at his difficulties, his tenacity—
still absorbed in the battle of good and evil,
he has seen a hundred prophets, and is an infidel yet.'

My soul in my body quivered for his agony;
a sigh of anguish broke from his lips.
With eyes half-closed he turned to me and said;
'Who besides me has so gloried in action?
I have become so involved in labour
that even on the sabbath I am rarely at rest,
I have no angels, no servants attending me;
my revelation is without benefit of prophets.
I have brought neither Traditions nor Book;
I have robbed theologians of their sweet soul.
None ever spun finer than they the thread of religion,
yet in the end they left the Kaaba a heap of bricks.
My religion has no such foundation;
in the faith of Iblis there are no schisms and sects.
Ignorant one, I have given up prostration,

I have turned the organ of good and evil.
Do not take me for one who denies God's existence;
open your eyes on my inner self, overlook my exterior.
If I say, "He is not", that would be foolishness,
for when one has seen, one cannot say, "He is not".
Under the veil of "No" I murmured "Yes";
what I have spoken is better than what I never said.
To share in the pain and suffering of Adam
I did not forgo the fury of the Beloved.
Flames sprang forth from my sown field;
man out of predestination achieved free-will.
I displayed my own hideousness
and have given you the joy of leaving or choosing.
Deliver me now from my fire;
resolve, O man, the knot of my toil.
You who have fallen into my noose
and given to Satan the leave to disobey,
live in the world with true manly zeal;
as you pity me, live a stranger to me
proudly disregarding my sting and my honey,
so that my scroll may not become blacker still.
In the world the huntsman lives on his prey;
whilst you are my prey, I draw out my arrows.
He who soars aloft is secure from falling:
if the quarry is cunning, the huntsman will fail.'

'Give up this cult of separation', I said to him.
'The most hateful of things to God is divorce.'
He said, 'The fire of separation is the stuff of life;
how sweet the intoxication of the day of separation!
The very name of union comes not to my lips;
if I seek union, neither He remains nor I.'
The word 'union' made him out of himself;
the burning agony was renewed in his heart.
He wallowed awhile in his own fumes,
he became lost again in his own fumes;
out of those fumes whirling a lament rose high;
how blessed the soul that can feel anguish!

God of the righteous and the unrighteous,
man's company has devastated me.
Not once has he rebelled against my rule;
he has closed his eyes to himself, and has not found himself.
His dust is a stranger to the joy of disobedience,
a stranger to the spark of pride.
The prey says to the huntsman, 'Seize me':
save me from the all too obedient servant!
Set me free from such a quarry;
remember my obedience of yesterday.
My lofty aspiration through him has been abased;
alas for me, alas for me, alas for me!
His nature is raw, his resolution weak,
this opponent cannot withstand one blow from me.
I need a servant of God possessed of vision,
I need a riper adversary!
Take back this plaything of water and clay:
a child's toy suits not a man of a certain age.
What is man? A handful of straw;
one spark from me is enough for a handful of straw.
If nothing but straw existed in this world,
what profited it to endow me with so much fire?
It were a shame to melt a piece of glass;
to melt a rock—that is a proper task!
I have become so saddened by all my triumphs
that now I come to You for recompense;
I seek from You one who dares to deny me—
guide me, to such a man of God.
I need a man who will twist my neck,
whose glance will set my body quivering,
one who will say, 'Depart from my presence',
one in whose eyes I am not worth two barleycorns.
Grant me, O God, one living man of faith;
haply I shall know delight at last in defeat.

THE SPHERE OF SATURN

The vile spirits which have betrayed the nation and have been rejected by Hell

The Sage of Rum, leader of the righteous,
familiar with all the stages of the righteous,
spoke: 'Hard-toiling traveller of the heavens,
do you see yonder world that wears a girdle?
That which it has twisted around its waist
it stole from the tail of a star.
So heavy of pace it is, its motion seems stationary;
under its rule, every good is turned to evil and base.
Though its form is fashioned of water and clay
it is difficult to set foot on its soil.
A myriad angels, thunder in hand,
dispensing God's wrath since the Day of Alast,
continually castigate the planet
and dislodge it from its pivot.
A world rejected and repelled by heaven,
its morn is as evening, the sun is so grudging.
It is the lodging-place of spirits that shall know no resurrection,
which Hell itself shrank from burning:
therein live two ancient demons
who slew a people's soul to save their skins,
Jaafar of Bengal and Sadiq of Deccan,
shame to mankind, religion and fatherland,
unaccepted, despairing, undesired,
a nation ruined by their handiwork.
A nation, which had loosed the bonds of every nation,
thus lost its high sovereignty and its faith.
Do you not know that the land of India,
dear to the heart of every sensitive soul,

a land whose every manifestation lit up the world,
now grovels amid dust and blood?
Who sowed in its soil the seed of slavery?
All this is the handiwork of those evil spirits.
Pause a moment in the azure expanse
that you may see the retribution for their deeds.

The Sea of Blood

What I beheld was indescribable;
body by terror was dissundered from soul.
What met my eyes? A sea of blood I viewed
tempest-torn outwardly and inwardly;
the air swarmed with snakes, as with sharks the sea,
their hoods black as night, their pinions quicksilver;
billows roaring and rending like panthers
so that the sharks in terror of them lay dead on the shore.
The sea gave the shore not one moment's respite;
every instant mountain-blocks fell crashing in blood.
Bloody wave fought with wave of blood,
whilst in their midst a skiff tossed up and down;
in that skiff were two men pale of cheek,
pale of cheek, naked, with hair dishevelled.

The Spirit of India appears

Heaven split in twain. A pure-born houri
lifted the veil from her countenance;
on her brow shone eternal fire and light,
her eyes were radiant with immortal joy.
The robe covering her was lighter than a cloud,
its warp and woof of the veins of rose-petals.
With all such loveliness, she was doomed to chains and fetters,
and from her lips sighs of agony broke.
Rumi said, 'See, this is the Spirit of India;
the heart is broken by her lamentation.'

The Spirit of India laments

The soul's candle is quenched in the lamp of India:
Indians are strangers to India's fair repute,
its manikins not intimate with their self's secrets,
their plectrum plucks but rarely at their strings.
They fasten their eyes upon the past,
their hearts would glow from an extinguished fire.
Because of them I am bound hand and foot,
they are the reason for my unavailing laments;
they have estranged themselves from their selfhood,
they have made a prison of ancient customs.
Humanity is pained by their existence:
the new age is outraged by their 'clean' and 'unclean'.

Have done with the poverty that bestows nakedness;
blessed is the poverty which bestows true power.
Beware of constraint and of the habit of patience;
constraint is poison to both constrainer and constrained—
the latter becomes habituated to patience,
the former becomes habituated to constraint;
for both the pleasure of oppression increases
and I can only repeat, *Ah, would that my people knew*!
When shall India's night give place to day?
Jaafar is dead, but his spirit is living still;
as soon as it escapes from the chains of one body
at once it makes its nest in another flesh.
Now it makes concord with the church,
anon it turns entreating to the templars;
its creed, its cult are nothing but commerce,
an Antar got up in the robes of Haidar.
As the world changes in scent and colour,
even so its customs and usages change;
In former times it bowed before other gods,
in our days its idol is the fatherland.
Outwardly it is anguished for the Faith,
inwardly it wears the thread like the templars.
Jaafar, in whatever body, murders the nation;
this 'good old Moslem' murders the nation.

He is always smiling, and is friends with none;
let a snake smile, it is still a snake.
His treachery divided the people's unity;
his nation is demeaned by the fact of his being.
Whenever a nation is devastated
the root of its ruin is a Sadiq or a Jaafar.
God save me from the spirit of Jaafar,
save me from the Jaafars of the present time!

The lament of one of the skiff-riders of the Sea of Blood

Neither not-being nor being will accept us:
alas, for the unkindness of being and not-being!
We passed through the world of East and West
and with pain and affliction reached the gates of Hell,
but Hell shot not a single spark at Sadiq and Jaafar
nor even a handful of ashes hurled at our heads,
saying, 'Sticks and straws are better for Hell;
my flame is better unsullied by these two infidels.'

We journeyed beyond the nine heavens
seeking to come to sudden death
which spoke: 'The soul is a secret among my secrets;
it is my task to preserve the soul and destroy the body.
Though the wicked soul is not worth two barleycorns,
be gone, you who would have me destroy the soul!
Such a task cannot be performed by Death;
the traitor's soul will not find rest in Death.'
Swift winds! O sea of blood,
O earth, O azure heaven,
O stars, O shining moon, O sun!
O Pen, O Preserved Tablet, O Book!
White idols! Lords of the West,
who hold a world in your grip without war and violence!
This world without beginning is without end;
where is the Lord Protector of traitors?

Suddenly there came a terrible sound
which split the breast of desert and ocean.
The whole realm of body disjointed fell apart;
moment by moment the mountain-masses crumbled—
mountains like clouds in motion—
a world's destruction without the Blast of the Trumpet.
Lightning and thunder, fired by an inward fever,
sought a nest of refuge in the Sea of Blood.
The billows boiled and broke out of themselves;
mountains and valleys were drowned in blood.
All that befell the visible and the invisible
the stars' cavalcade beheld, and passed on indifferently.

BEYOND THE SPHERES

The station of the German philosopher Nietzsche

The conflict of being and not-being is universal;
no man knows the secret of yon azure sky.
Everywhere death brings the message of life—
happy is the man who knows what death is.
Everywhere life is as cheap as the wind,
unstable, and aspiring to stability.
My eyes had beheld a hundred six-day worlds
and at last the borders of this universe appeared;
each world had a different moon, a different Pleiades,
a different manner and mode of existence.
Time in each world flowed like the sea,
here slowly, and there swiftly;
our year was here a month, there a moment,
this world's more was that world's less.
Our reason in one world was all-cunning,
in another world it was mean and abased.

On the frontiers of this world of quality and quantity
dwelt a man with a voice full of agony,
his vision keener than an eagle's,
his mien witness to a heart afire;
every moment his inward glow increased.
On his lips was a verse he chanted a hundred times:
'No Gabriel, no Paradise, no houri, no God,
only a handful of dust consumed by a yearning soul.'

I said to Rumi, 'Who is this madman?'
He answered: 'This is the German genius

whose place is between these two worlds;
his reed-pipe contains an ancient melody.
This Hallaj without gallows and rope
has spoken anew those ancient words;
his words are fearless, his thoughts sublime,
the Westerners are struck asunder by the sword of his speech.
His colleagues have not comprehended his ecstasy
and have reckoned the ecstatic mad.
Intellectuals have no share of love and intoxication;
they placed his pulse in the hand of the physician,
yet what have doctors but deceit and fraud?
Alas for the ecstatic born in Europe!
Avicenna puts his faith in textbooks
and slits a vein, or prescribes a sleeping-pill.
He was a Hallaj who was a stranger in his own city;
he saved his life from the mullahs, and the physicians slew him.

'There was none in Europe who knew the Way,
so his melody outstretched the strings of his lute;
none showed the wayfarer the road,
and a hundred flaws vitiated his visitations.
He was true coin, but there was none to assay him,
expert in theory, but none to prove him;
a lover lost in the labyrinth of his sighs,
a traveller gone astray in his own path.
His intoxication shattered every glass;
he broke from God, and was snapped too from himself.
He desired to see, with his external eyes,
the intermingling of power with love;
he yearned for these to come forth from water and clay
a cluster sprouting from the seed-bud of the heart.
What he was seeking was the station of Omnipotence,
which station transcends reason and philosophy.
Life is a commentary on the hints of the Self,
"no" and "but" are of the stations of the Self;
he remained fast in "no" and did not reach "but"

being a stranger to the station of "His servant".
Revelation embraced him, yet he knew it not,
being like fruit all the farther from the roots of the tree.
His eyes desired no other vision but man;
fearlessly he shouted, "Where is man?"
and else he had despaired of earth's creatures
and like Moses he was seeking the vision.
Would that he had lived in Ahmad's time,
so that he might have attained eternal joy.
His reason is in dialogue with itself;
take your own way, for one's own way is good.
Stride onwards, for now that station has come
wherein speech sprouts without spoken words.'

Departure for the Garden of Paradise

I passed beyond the bounds of this universe
and set foot in the undimensioned world,
a world without both right and left,
a world devoid of night and day.
Before it the lantern of my perception dimmed,
my words died in awe of the meaning.
To speak of the spirit with the tongue of water and clay—
it is very hard to soar in a cage!

Regard a little while the world of the heart
that you may win clear vision by the light of the Self.
What is the heart? A world without colour and scent,
a world without colour and scent and without dimensions.
The heart is at rest, yet every moment in motion;
the heart is a world of spiritual states and thoughts.
Reason makes its way from fact to fact,
it travels without highroad and tramping and transport;
a hundred images, each different from the other,
this one acquaint with heaven, that one unattaining.
No one says that this which is acquaint with heaven

is on the right hand of that unattaining image,
or that the joy which comes from beholding the Beloved
is but half a pace from the air of His street.
Your eyes may be wakeful or asleep;
the heart sees without the rays of the sun.
Know that world by the world of the heart—
yet what shall I say of what defies analogy?

In that universe was another world
whose origin was from another Divine fiat,
undecaying, and every moment transformed,
unimaginable, yet there clearly visible;
every moment clothed in a new perfection,
every moment clad in a new beauty.
Its time had no need of moon and sun;
in its expanse the nine spheres are contained.
Whatever is in the Unseen comes face to face
even before the desire for it issues from the heart.
How can I tell in my own tongue what it is,
this world? It is light, and presence, and life.
Tulips repose amidst the mountains,
rivers meander in the rose-gardens;
buds crimson, white and blue
blossom with the breath of the holy ones;
its waters silver, the air ambergris,
palaces with domes of emerald,
tents of ruby with golden ropes,
beauties with countenances radiant as a mirror.
Rumi said, 'Prisoner of analogy,
pass beyond the credibility of the senses,
acts fair and foul derive out of manifestation,
the latter turning to Hell, the former to Heaven;
these many-coloured palaces you behold
are built of deeds, not of bricks and stones;
what you call Kauthar and page and houri
are the reflection of this world of ecstasy and joy.
Here life is the Beatific Vision, naught else,
the bliss of seeing and speaking with the Beloved.'

I said, 'Yonder mansion of pure ruby
which gathers tribute from the sun,
yon station, yon abode, yon lofty palace
whose portico the houris throng pilgrim-robed—
tell me, you who inspired the travellers to search,
who is the owner of this habitation?'
Rumi replied: 'This is the mansion of Sharaf al-Nisa;
the birds on its roof sing in the angels' choir.
Our ocean gave not birth to such a pearl;
no mother gave birth to such a daughter.
By her grave the earth of Lahore vies with heaven;
none in this world comprehends her secret.
She was all ecstasy and yearning, anguish and burning,
eyes and lamp to the governor of Panjab;
radiance of the family of Abd al-Samad,
her poverty is an image remaining eternally.
To cleanse her being wholly with the Koran,
not for one moment did she cease recitation;
at her side a double-edged sword, the Koran in her hand,
flesh, body, mind and soul drunken with God;
solitude with sword, Koran and prayer—
O happy life, passed in supplication!
When the last breath issued from her lips,
looking upon her mother most yearningly
she spoke: "If you would have knowledge of my secret,
regard this sword and this Koran.
These two forces preserve each the other
and are the axis of all life's creation.
In this world, which dies every moment,
only these two were your daughter's intimates.
Now that I take my leave I have this to say to you:
do not remove the sword and the Koran from me.
Take to your heart these words I speak;
better my tomb without dome and lamp;
for believers, sword and Koran suffice—
let this be the furniture of my grave."

For long ages, beneath this golden dome,

the sword and the scriptures lay upon her shrine.
Her resting-place, in this inconstant world,
spoke a message to the people of the Truth
until the Moslems did with themselves what they did
and time's revolution rolled up their carpet.
The man of God was mindful of other than God,
the lion of the Lord took to the trade of the fox;
the quicksilver fire and fever departed from his heart—
you know well what befell Panjab—
the Khalsa snatched away sword and Koran
and in that land Islam expired.'

Visitation to His Highness Sayyid Ali Hamadani and Mulla Tahir Ghani of Kashmir

Rumi's words kindled a fire in my heart.
Alas for Panjab, that precious land!
Even in Paradise I burned with the fever
of my friends, and knew again my ancient griefs
until in that bower a sorrowful voice
rose up from the banks of the stream Kauthar:
'I gathered a handful of straw to set myself on fire;
the rose supposes that I would build a nest in the garden.'

Rumi said, 'Observe what is now coming;
give not your heart to what has passed, my son.
That poet of colourful song, Tahir Ghani,
whose poverty abounds in riches inward and outward,
drunk with eternal wine, is chanting a melody
in the presence of the Sayyid sublime,
noble of nobles, commander of Persia,
whose hand is the architect of the destiny of nations.
Ghazali himself learned the lesson of *God is He*
and drew meditation and thought from his stock.
Guide he of that emerald land,
counsellor of prince and dervish and sultan;
a king ocean-munificent, to that vale

he gave science, crafts, education, religion.
That man created a miniature Iran
with rare and heart-ravishing arts;
with one glance he unravels a hundred knots—
rise, and let his arrow transfix your heart.'

In the presence of Shah-i Hamadan
Zinda-Rud

I seek from you the key to the secret of God:
He sought from us obedience, and created Satan.
So to adorn the hideous and unlovely
and to demand of us comeliness of works—
I ask you, what is this magic-mongering,
what this dicing with an evil adversary?
A handful of dust, against yon revolving sphere—
tell me now, did it beseem Him so to do?
Our labour, our thoughts, our anguish
is but to bite our hands in despair.

Shah-i Hamadan

The man who is fully aware of himself
creates advantage out of loss.
To sup with the Devil brings disaster to a man,
to wrestle with the Devil brings him glory.
One must strike oneself against Ahriman;
you are a sword, he is the whetstone;
become sharper, that your stroke may be hard,
else you will be unfortunate in both worlds.

Zinda-Rud

Under the heavens man devours man,
nation grazes upon another nation.
My soul burns like rue for the people of the Vale;

cries of anguish mount from my heart.
They are a nation clever, perceptive, handsome,
their dexterity is proverbial,
yet their cup rolls in their own blood;
the lament in my flute is on their behalf.
Since they have lost their share of selfhood
they have become strangers in their own land;
their wages are in the hands of others,
the fish of their river in other men's nets.
The caravans move step by step to the goal;
but still their work is ill-done, unformed, immature.
Through servitude their aspirations have died,
the fire in the veins of their vine is quenched.
But do not think that they were always so,
their brows ever lowered thus to the dust;
once upon a time they too were warlike folk,
valiant, heroic, ardent in battle.

Behold her mountains turbaned in white,
behold the fiery hands of her chenars;
in springtime rubies leap down from the rocks,
a flood of colour rises from her soil,
stippled clouds cover mountain and valley
like cotton-flocks strewn from a carder's bow.
Mountain and river, and the setting of the sun:
there I behold God without a veil.
I wandered with the zephyr in Nishat
chanting as I roved, 'Listen to the reed'.
A bird perched in the branches was singing:
'This springtide is not worth a penny.
The tulip has blossomed, the dark-eyed narcissus is in bloom,
the breeze of Nauruz has torn their skirts;
for many ages from this mountain and valley have sprung
daisies purer than the light of the moon,
for many ages the rose has packed and unpacked her baggage,
yet our earth has not begotten a second Shihab al-Din.'

The passionate lament of that bird of dawn
filled my heart with new fire and fever.
Presently I beheld a madman, whose threnody
robbed me of all endurance and reason.

'Pass us by, and seek not an impassioned lament,
pass from the rose-twig, that talisman of colour and scent.
You said that dew was dripping from the tulip's petals;
nay, it is a feckless heart weeping beside the river.
What have these few feathers to do with such a chant?
It is the spirit of Ghani mourning the death of desire.
Zephyr, if you should pass over Geneva
speak a word from me to the League of Nations:
they have sold farmer and cornfield, river and garden,
they have sold a people, and at a price how cheap.'

Shah-i Hamadan

I will tell you a subtle mystery, my son:
the body is all clay, the soul a precious pearl.
The body must be melted for the sake of the soul,
the pure must be distinguished from the clay.
If you cut off a part of the body from the body,
that slice of the body will be lost to you;
but the soul which is drunk with vision—
if you give it away, it will return to you.
The soul's substance resembles nothing else;
it is in bonds, and yet not in bonds;
if you watch over it, it dies in the body,
and if you scatter it, it illuminates the gathering.
What, noble sir, is the soul 'drunk with vision'?
What does it mean to 'give the soul away'?
To give away the soul is to surrender it to God,
it means melting the mountain with the soul's flame.
'Drunk with vision' means discovering one's self,
shining like a star in the night-season:
not to discover one's self is not to exist,
to discover is to bestow the self on the Self.

Whosoever has seen himself and has seen naught else
has drawn forth the load from the self's prison;
the 'drunk with vision' who beholds himself
deems the sting sweeter than the honey—
in his eyes the soul is cheap as the air,
before him the walls of his prison tremble;
his axe shivers the granite rock
so that he takes his share of the universe.
When he gives up the soul, his soul is truly his,
otherwise his soul is his guest but for a moment or two.

Zinda-Rud

You have spoken of the wisdom of foul and fair;
learned sage, expound a further subtlety.
You were the guide of those who behold the inner meaning,
you were the confidant of the secrets of kings.
We are poor men, and the ruler demands tribute;
what is the origin of the sanction of throne and crown?

Shah-i Hamadan

What is the origin of Kingship in East and West?
Either the consent of the peoples, or war and violence.
Exalted sir, I will speak with you plainly;
it is forbidden to pay tribute save to two persons:
either *those in authority* as being *among you*,
whose proof and demonstration is the verse of God,
or else a hero swift-rising like a hurricane
who seizes cities, and stakes himself in the battle,
on the day of war conquering the land by force of arms,
on the day of peace by the winning ways of love.
You might indeed purchase Iran and India,
but kingship cannot be bought from any man;
virtuous friend, the Cup of Jamshid
none shall procure from the glassmaker's shop,
or if he procures aught, all he owns is glass,
and glass has no other property but to break.

Who gave to India this yearning for freedom?
Who gave the quarry this passion to be the hunter?
Those scions of Brahmins, with vibrant hearts,
whose glowing cheeks put the red tulip to shame—
keen of eye, mature and strenuous in action
whose very glance puts Europe into commotion.
Their origin is from this protesting soil of ours,
the rising-place of these stars is our Kashmir.
If you suppose our earth is without a spark,
cast a glance for a moment within your heart;
whence comes all this ardour you possess,
whence comes this breath of the breeze of spring?
It is from the selfsame wind's influence
that our mountains derive their colour and scent.

Do you not know what one day a wave
said to another wave in Lake Wular?
'How long shall we strike at each other in this sea?
Rise up, let us break together against the shore.
Our child, that is to say, yon ancient river
fills with its roar valley and mountains and meadow;
continually it smites the rocks on its path
until it uproots the fabric of the mountains.
That youth who seized cities, deserts and plains
took his nurture from the milk of a hundred mothers;
its majesty strikes terror into mortal hearts;
all this is from us, not from any other.
To live in the bounds of the shore is a sin;
our shore is but a stone in our path.
To accommodate oneself to the shore is eternal death,
even though you roll in the sea morning and evening;
life is to leap amidst mountain and desert—
happy is the wave that has transgressed the shore!'

You who have read the lines on the brow of Life,
you who have given to the East the tumult of Life,

you who have a sigh that consumes the heart,
stirring you to restlessness, and us still more,
from you the birds in the meadow learned their threnody,
in your tears the grasses make ablution;
out of your genius the field of roses blossomed,
out of your hope many souls are filled with hope.
Your cry is a bell urging the caravans;
why then do you despair of the dwellers in the Vale?
Their hearts are not dead in their breasts,
their embers are not extinguished under the ice;
wait till you see, without the sound of the Trumpet,
a nation rising out of the dust of the tomb.
Do not grieve then, visionary;
breathe out that sigh consuming all, dry and moist alike;
many cities beneath the turquoise heaven
have been consumed by the flame of a dervish heart.
Dominion is frailer than a bubble
and can be destroyed by a single breath.
The destinies of nations have been shaped by a song,
by a song nations are destroyed and rebuilt.
Though your lancet has pierced men's hearts,
none has perceived you as you truly are;
your melody springs from a poet's song,
but what you utter transcends poesy.
Stir up a new tumult in Paradise,
strike up an intoxicating air in Paradise!

Zinda-Rud

Habituate yourself to the dervish wine and quaff it continuously;
when you become riper, hurl yourself at the dominion of Jamshid.
They said, 'This world of ours—does it agree with you?'
I said, 'It does not agree'. They said, 'Then break it to pieces'.
In the taverns I have seen there is not one worthy adversary;
grapple with Rustam-i Dastan, have done with Magian boys!
Tulip of the wilderness, you cannot burn alone;

strike this heart-enflaming brand upon the breast of man;
You are the ardour of his bosom, the heat of his blood—
do you not believe me? Then tear apart the flesh of the world.
Is reason your lamp? Set it on the path to shine;
or is love your cup? Quaff it with the intimate.
I pour forth from my eyes the bloody gouts of my heart;
my ruby of Badakhshan—pick it up, and set it in your ring.

Meeting with the Indian poet Bartari-Hari

The houris in their palaces and pavilions
my lament provoked to supreme ardour;
one here put forth her head from her tent,
another there peeped out from her chamber and gazed;
to every heart in eternal Paradise
I gave of the pain and sorrow of yon terrestrial globe.
A smile played on the lips of my holy guide
and he said: 'O magician of Indian stock,
behold now that Indian minstrel
the grace of whose gaze converts the dew to pearls.
a broiderer of subtleties, his name is Bartari,
his nature generous as the clouds of Azar;
from the meadow he plucks only the new-sprung buds.
Your melody has drawn him towards us,
a king who, with a song sublime,
even in poverty dwells in lofty exaltation;
with his delicate thought he designs images of beauty,
a whole world of meaning hidden in two words.
He is intimate with the workshop of life,
he is Jamshid, his poetry Jamshid's Cup.'
We rose in reverence for his art
and prepared suitably to engage with him.

Zinda-Rud

You who have uttered heart-delighting subtleties,
through whose discourse the East knows all mysteries,

say, whence comes the fire into poetry?
Does it come from the Self, or from God?

Bartari-Hari

None knows where the poet is in this world;
his melody springs from the high notes and the low.
That burning heart which he has in his breast
finds not repose even before God.
Our soul's delight is in questing;
poetry's fire is of the station of desire.
You who are drunk with wine pressed from the vine of words,
if you should ever attain to this rank,
with two verses in this world of stone and brick
one can ravish the hearts of the houris of Paradise.

Zinda-Rud

I have seen the Indians twisting this way and that;
it is time you told the secret of God unveiled.

Bartari-Hari

These frail gods are but of stone and brick;
there is One more lofty, far from temple and church.
Prostration without the joy of action is dry and useless;
life is all action, whether fair or foul.
I will tell you plainly a word not known to every one—
happy is the man who has written it on his heart's tablet.
This world you behold is not the handiwork of God,
the wheel is yours, and the thread spun on your spindle.
Prostrate yourself before the Law of action's reward,
for from action are born Hell, Purgatory and Paradise.

Departure to the palace of the kings of the East,
Nadir, Abdali, the Martyr-King

The voice of Bartari penetrated into my soul;
I was intoxicated with Bartari's song.

Rumi said: 'It is better to open your eyes,
better to step outside the circle of your thoughts.
You have passed by the banquet of dervishes;
give one glance also at the palace of kings.
The sovereigns of the East are here assembled,
the might of Iran, Afghanistan and Deccan—
Nadir, who knew the secret of unity
and conveyed to the Moslems the message of love;
heroic Abdali, his whole being a sign,
who gave the Afghans the foundation of nationhood;
that leader of all the martyrs of love,
"glory of India, China, Turkey and Syria",
whose name is more resplendent than the sun and the moon,
the dust of whose grave is more living than I and you.
Love is a mystery, which he revealed in the open plain—
do you not know how yearningly he gave his life?
By grace of the gaze of the victor of Badr and Hunain
the poverty of the king became heir to Husain's ecstasy;
the King departed from this tavern of seven days,
yet still to this day his trumpet sounds in Deccan.'

My words and voice are immature, my thought imperfect:
how can I hope to describe that place?
The beings of light from its reflected glory derive vision,
vitality, knowledge, speech, awareness;
a palace whose walls and gates are of turquoise
holding in its bosom the whole azure sky;
soaring beyond the bounds of quantity and quality,
it reduces thought to mean impotence.
The roses, the cypresses, the jasmines, the flowering boughs
delicate as a picture painted by the hand of spring;
the petals of the flowers, the leaves of the trees every moment
put on new colours out of the joy of growth—
such a spellbinder the zephyr is
that as you wink, gold is turned to scarlet;

on every side pearl-scattering fountains,
birds born of Paradise in clamant song.
Within that lofty palace was a chamber
whose motes held the sun in a lasso;
the roof, walls and columns were of red agate,
the floor of jasper, enclosed in carnation.
To the right and left of that lodge
houris with golden girdles stood in ranks,
and in the midst, seated on thrones of gold,
sovereigns stately as Jamshid, splendid as Bahram.
Rumi, that mirror of perfect refinement,
with utmost affection opened his lips
saying, 'Here is a poet from the East—
either a poet, or an eastern magician;
his thoughts are acute, his soul impassioned;
his verses have kindled a fire in all the East'.

Nadir

Welcome to you, eastern weaver of subtleties
whose lips the Persian speech so well beseems!
We are your intimate friends; tell us your secret,
reveal what you know of Iran.

Zinda-Rud

After long ages she opened her eyes on herself,
but then she fell into the snare of a trap,
slain by the charm of bold and elegant idols,
creator of culture—and slavish imitation of Europe.
Lost in the cult of 'rulership' and 'race', she acclaims
the glory of Shapur, and despises the Arabs;
her day today being empty of new achievements
she seeks for life in ancient sepulchres.
Wedded to the 'fatherland', having abandoned her self
she has given her heart to Rustam, and turned from Haidar.
She is accepting a false image from Europe,
she takes the version of her history from Europe.

Iran was aged already in the time of Yazdajird,
her cheeks were lack-lustre, her blood was cold,
ancient her religion, her laws, her system,
ancient the light and dark of her dawn and eve;
in her vine's flask no wine foamed,
no spark glowed in her heap of dust,
till from the desert a resurrection came to her
which endowed her with new life.
Such a resurrection is a grace of God:
Persia lives on—where is Rome the mighty?
He from whose body the pure spirit has departed
cannot rise from the dust without a resurrection.
The desert-dwellers breathed life into Iran
and then sped back to their sandy wastes;
they erased from our tablet all that was old, and departed,
they brought the apparatus of a new age, and departed.
Alas, Iran has not recognized the benefaction of the Arabs;
she has melted away in Europe's fire.

The spirit of Nasir-i Khusrau Alavi appears, sings an impassioned ghazal, and vanishes

Once you have taken the sword in your hand and grasped the pen
do not grieve if your body's steed be lame or halt:
virtue is born of the edge of the sword, and the point of the pen,
my brother, as light from fire, and fire from narvan-tree.
Know, that to the faithless, both sword and pen are without virtue;
when faith is not, reed and steel have no worth.
Faith is precious to the wise, and to the ignorant it is contemptible;
before the ignorant, faith is like jasmine before a cow.
Faith is like fine linen, of which one half makes a shirt
for Elias, and the other half a shroud for a Jew.

Abdali

That youth who created dominions,
then fled back to his mountains and deserts,

kindled a fire on his mountain-peaks—
did he emerge of fine assay, or was he utterly consumed?

Zinda-Rud

Whilst other nations are eager in brotherhood,
with him brother is at war against brother.
From his life the life of the whole East derives;
his ten-year-old child is a leader of armies.
Yet ignorantly he has broken himself from himself,
not recognizing his own potentialities.
He possesses a heart, and is unaware of that heart;
body is parted from body, heart from heart;
a traveller, he has lost the road to the good,
his soul is unconscious of its true purposes.
Finely sang that poet familiar with Afghan,
who proclaimed fearlessly what he saw,
that sage of the Afghan nation,
that physician of the sickness of the Afghans;
he saw the people's secret, and boldly uttered
the word of truth with a drunkard's recklessness:
'If a free Afghan should find a camel
richly caparisoned and loaded with pearls,
his mean spirit, with all that load of pearls,
is only delighted with the camel-bell.'

Abdali

In our nature, fever and ardour spring from the heart;
waking and slumber possess the body from the heart.
When the heart dies, the body is transformed:
when the heart vies for glory, the sweat turns to blood.
The body is nothing, nothing, when the heart is corrupt;
so fix your eyes on the heart, and be attached to naught else.
Asia is a form cast of water and clay;
in that form the Afghan nation is the heart;
if it is corrupt, all Asia is corrupt,

if it is dilated, all Asia is dilated.
So long as the heart is free, the body is free,
else, the body is a straw in the path of the wind.
Like the body, the heart too is bound by laws—
the heart dies of hatred, lives of faith.
The power of faith derives from unity;
when unity becomes visible, it is a nation.

Imitation of the West seduces the East from itself;
these peoples have need to criticize the West.
The power of the West comes not from lute and rebeck,
not from the dancing of unveiled girls,
not from the magic of tulip-cheeked enchantresses,
not from naked legs and bobbed hair;
its solidity springs not from irreligion,
its glory derives not from the Latin script.
The power of the West comes from science and technology,
and with that selfsame flame its lamp is bright.
Wisdom derives not from the cut and trim of clothes;
the turban is no impediment to science and technology.
For science and technology, elegant young sprig,
brains are necessary, not European clothes;
on this road only keen sight is required,
what is needed is not this or that kind of hat.
If you have a nimble intellect, that is sufficient;
if you have a perceptive mind, that is sufficient.

If anyone burns the midnight oil
he will find the track of science and technology.
None has fixed the bounds of the realm of meaning
which is not attained without incessant effort.
The Turks have departed from their own selves, drunk with Europe,
having quaffed honeyed poison from the hand of Europe;
of those who have abandoned the antidote of Iraq

what shall I say, except 'God help them'?
The slave of Europe, eager to show off,
borrows from the Westerners their music and dances;
he gambles away his precious soul for frivolity—
science is a hard quest, so he makes do with fun.
Being slothful, he takes the easy way;
his nature readily accepts the easy alternative.
To seek for ease in this ancient convent
proves that the soul has gone out of the body.

Zinda-Rud

Do you know what European culture is?
In its world are two hundred paradises of colour;
its dazzling shows have burned down abodes,
consumed with fire branch, leaf and nest.
Its exterior is shining and captivating
but its heart is weak, a slave to the gaze;
the eye beholds, the heart staggers within
and falls headlong before this idol-temple.
No man knows what the East's destiny may be;
what is to be done with the heart bound to the exterior?

Abdali

What is able to control the East's destiny
is the unbending resolve of Pahlavi and Nadir:
Pahlavi, that heir to the throne of Qubad
whose nail has resolved the knot of Iran,
and Nadir, that sum-capital of the Durranis
who has given order to the Afghan nation.
Distressed on account of the Faith and Fatherland
his armies came forth from the mountains:
at once soldier, officer and Emir
steel with his enemies, silk with his friends—
let me be ransom for him who has seen his self
and has weighed well the present age!
The Westerners can have their magic tricks;
to rely on other than oneself is infidelity.

The Martyr-King

Speak again of the Indians and of India—
one blade of her grass no garden can outmatch;
speak of her in whose mosques the tumult has died,
of her in whose temples the fire is quenched,
of her for whose sake I gave my blood,
whose memory I have nursed in my soul.
From my grief you may guess at her grief;
alas, for the beloved who knows no more the lover!

Zinda-Rud

The Indians reject the statutes of Europe,
they are immune to Europe's magic charms;
alien laws are a heavy burden on the soul
even though they descend from heaven itself.

The Martyr-King

How man grows from a handful of dust
with a heart, and with desire in that heart!
His concern is to taste the delight of rebellion,
not to behold anything but himself;
for without rebellion the self is unattainable,
and while the self is not attained, defeat is inevitable.
You have visited my city and my land,
you have rubbed your eyes upon my tomb;
you who know the limits of all creation,
in Deccan have you seen any trace of life?

Zinda-Rud

I scattered the seeds of my tears in Deccan;
tulips are growing from the soil of that garden;
the river Cauvery unceasing on its journey—
in its soul I have beheld a new commotion.

You who have been endowed with heart-illumining words,
I burn still with the fever of your tears.
The incessant digging of the nails of the initiates
has opened a river of blood from the veins of the lute.
That melody which issues out of your soul
imparts to every breast an inward fire.
I was in the presence of the Lord of All,
without whom no path can be traversed;
though there none may dare to speak,
and the spirit's only occupation is to behold,
I was afire with the ardour of your verses
and some of your thoughts came on my tongue.
He said, 'Whose is this verse which you recited?
In it pulses the true vibration of life'.
With the same ardour, congenial to the soul,
convey from me one or two words to the Cauvery.
You, Zinda-Rud, 'living stream', he too a living stream—
sweeter sounds melody interwoven with melody.

Message of the Martyr-King to the River Cauvery

(The reality of life, death and martyrdom)

River Cauvery, flow gently for a while;
perchance you are wearied by continual wandering.
For many years you have wept in the mountains,
carving out your path with your eyelashes.
Sweeter to me than Oxus and Euphrates,
to Deccan your water is the Water of Life.
Alas, for the city which lay in your embrace,
whose sweet beauty was a reflection of your sweetness!
You have grown old, yet you are ever young,
ever the same your surge, your ardour, your lustre;
your waves have begotten only the purest pearls—
may your tresses flow freely till all eternity!
You whose music is the very fire of life,
do you know from whom this message comes?
From him whose mighty power you once encircled,

whose empire you reflected in your mirror,
by whose contriving deserts were turned to Paradise,
who wrought his image with his own blood,
whose dust is the goal of a hundred yearnings,
and with whose blood your waves surge still;
the man whose words were all action,
the one man awake, whilst the East slept.
You and I are waves of life's river;
every moment this universe changes,
for life is a perpetual revolution
since it is ever searching for a new world.
This flux is the warp and woof of life,
this flux the source of the joy of manifestation;
the highways like travellers are on a journey;
apparently at rest, secretly everywhere in motion—
the caravan, the camels, the desert, the palm-trees,
whatever you see, weeps for the pain of parting.
In the garden the rose is a guest of but a moment,
its hue and lustre a moment's experiment.
The season of the rose? Funeral and festival together,
buds in the breast, the rose's bier on the back.
I said to the tulip, 'Burn once again';
the tulip answered, 'You know not yet my secret,
Existence is constructed of sticks and straws;
what is the guerdon of manifestation, but regret?'

Do you enter the inn of existence? Do not;
do you come from not-being to being? Do not,
or if you do, go not out of your self like a spark,
but become a wanderer searching for a stack to fire.
If you have fever and flame like the sun,
step forth into the vastness of the sky;
burn up mountain and bird, garden and desert,
burn even the fishes in the depths of the sea.
If you have a breast worthy of an arrow,
live like a falcon, and like a falcon die;
immortality is in the breadth of life—
I do not ask of God for length of days,

What is the law, the religion, the rite of life?
Better one instant a lion, than a century a sheep.

Life is fortified by cheerful resignation;
death is a magic talisman, a fantasy.
The man of God is a lion, and death a fawn;
death is but one station for him of a hundred.
The perfect man swoops upon death
even as a falcon swooping upon a dove,
The slave dies every moment in fear of death;
the fear of death makes life for him a thing forbidden;
the free servant has another dignity,
death bestows upon him a new life.
He is anxious for the self, but not for death,
since to the free death is no more than an instant.
Transcend the death that is content with the grave,
for that death is the death of brute beasts;
the true believer prays to the Holy God
for that other death which raises up from the dust.
That other death—the goal of the road of love,
the final Allahu Akbar in love's battlefield.
Though to the believer every death is sweet,
the death of Murtada's son is something other.
The warfare of worldly kings is for rapine,
the believer's warfare is the Sunna of the Prophet.
What is the believer's warfare? Flight to the Beloved;
quitting the world, choosing the Beloved's street,
He who proclaimed to the peoples the word of love
said of warfare that it was 'the monasticism of Islam'.
None but the martyr knows this subtlety,
for he has purchased this subtlety with his blood.

Zinda-Rud departs form Paradise: the Houris' request

The glass of my patience and quietude was shattered;
The Sage of Rum spoke in my ear, 'Rise up'.
Ah, those words of love, that ecstatic certainty!

Ah that court, that sublime palace;
heart bleeding, I reached its gate
and beheld there a throng of houris,
on their lips, 'Zinda-Rud, Zinda-Rud,
Zinda-Rud, master of fire and melody!'
Clamour and tumult rose from left and right:
'One or two moments sit with us, sit with us!'

Zinda-Rud

The traveller who knows the secrets of the journey
fears the lodging-place more than the highwayman.
Love reposes not in separation, nor in union,
reposes not, without Eternal Beauty;
first beginning, falling down before idols,
final end, freedom from all heart-ravishers.
Love recks for nothing, and is ever on the move,
a wayfarer in space and spacelessness.
Our creed, like the swift-paced wave:
abandon the halting-place, choose the highway.

The Houris of Paradise

Your blandishments are like those of Time;
grudge us not now one sweet song.

Ghazal of Zinda-Rud

You have not reached Man, so why do you seek God?
You have fled from your self; why do you seek a friend?
Hang again on the rose-twig and suck in the sap and the dew;
faded blossom, what are you seeking from the zephyr?
What they call musk is two drops of the heart's blood;
gazelle of the Sanctuary, what are you seeking in Cathay?
Poverty's assay is by sovereignty and world-dominion;

seek Jamshid's throne—why do you seek a reed-mat?
Men track it out from the garden of tulips;
why do you seek from me the song drenched with blood?
The vision augments through the company of the enlightened of heart;
why do you seek collyrium from the sorrow of the short-sighted?
We are calenders, and our miracle is world-vision;
seek vision from us—why seek the philosopher's stone?

The Divine Presence

Though Paradise is a manifestation of Him
the soul reposes not, save in the vision of Him.
We are veiled from our Origin;
we are as birds who have lost our nest.
If knowledge is perverse and evil of substance
it is the greatest curtain before our eyes;
but if the object of knowledge is contemplation
it becomes at once the highway and the guide,
laying bare before you the shell of being
that you may ask, 'What is the secret of this display?'
Thus it is that knowledge smoothes the road,
thus it is that it awakens desire;
it gives you pain and anguish, fire and fever,
it gives you midnight lamentations.
From the science of the interpretation of the world of colour and scent
your eyes and your heart derive nourishment;
it brings you to the stage of ecstasy and yearning
and then suffers you like Gabriel to stand.
How shall love bring any soul to the Solitude,
seeing love is jealous of its own eyes?
Its beginning is the road and the companion,
its end, travelling the road without companion.

I passed on from all the houris and palaces
and hazarded the soul's skiff on the sea of light.

I was drowned in the contemplation of Beauty,
which is constantly in eternal revolution;
I became lost in the heart of creation
till life appeared to me like a rebeck
whose every string was another lute,
each melody more blood-drenched than the other.
We are all one family of fire and light,
man, sun and moon, Gabriel and houri.
Before the soul a mirror has been hung,
bewilderment mingled with certainty;
today's dawn, whose light is manifest,
in His Presence is yesterday and tomorrow ever present.
God, revealed in all His mysteries,
with my eyes makes vision of Himself.
To see Him is to wax ever without waning,
to see Him is to rise from the body's tomb;
servant and Master lying in wait on one another,
each impatiently yearning to behold the other.
Life, wherever it may be, is a restless search;
unresolved is this riddle—am I the quarry, or is He?

Love gave my soul the delight of beholding,
gave my tongue the boldness to speak:
Thou who givest light and vision to both worlds,
look a little while on yonder ball of clay.
Uncongenial to the free servitor,
from its hyacinths springs the sting of thorns.
The victors are drowned in pleasure and enjoyment,
the vanquished have only to count the days and nights.
Thy world has been wasted by imperialism,
dark night ravelled in the sleeve of the sun.
The science of Westerners is spoliation;
the temples have turned to Khaibar, without a Haidar.
He who proclaims 'No god but God' is helpless;
his thought, having no centre, wanders astray,
slowly dying, pursued by four deaths—
the usurer, the governor, the mullah, the shaikh.
How is such a world worthy of Thee?
Water and clay are a stain upon Thy skirt.'

The Voice of Beauty

The Pen of God such images fair and foul
wrote exactly as became each one of us.
Noble sir, do you know what it is, to be?
It is to take one's share of the beauty of God's Essence.
Creating? It is to search for a beloved,
to display one's self to another being.
All these tumultuous riots of being
without our beauty could not come to exist.
Life is both transient and everlasting;
all this is creativity and vehement desire.
Are you alive? Be vehement, be creative;
like Us, embrace all horizons;
break whatsoever is uncongenial,
out of your heart's heart produce a new world—
it is irksome to the free servitor
to live in a world belonging to others.
Whoever possesses not the power to create
in Our sight is naught but an infidel, a heathen;
such a one has not taken his share of Our Beauty,
has not tasted the fruit of the Tree of Life.
Man of God, be trenchant as a sword,
be yourself your own world's destiny!

Zinda-Rud

What law governs the world of colour and scent,
but that water once flowed returns not to the stream?
Life has no desire for repetition,
its nature is not habituated to repetition;
beneath the sky, reversion is unlawful to life—
once a people has fallen, it rises not again.
When a nation dies, it rarely rises from the grave;
what recourse has it, but the tomb and resignation?

The Voice of Beauty

Life is not a mere repetition of the breath,
its origin is from the Living, Eternal God.

The soul near to Him who said 'Lo, I am nigh'—
that is to take one's share of everlasting life.
The individual through the Unity becomes Divine,
the nation through the Unity becomes Omnipotent;
Unity produced Ba Yazid, Shibli, Bu Dharr,
Unity produced, for the nations, Tughril and Sanjar.
Without the Divine Epiphany man has no permanence;
Our Manifestation is life to individual and nation;
both attain their perfection through the Unity,
life being for the latter Majesty, for the former Beauty.
The one is of Solomon, the other of Salman,
the one perfect poverty, the other all power:
the one sees there is One, the other becomes one—
while in the world, sit with the former, live with the latter!
What is the nation, you who declare 'No god but God'?
With thousands of eyes, to be one in vision.
The proof and claim of God's people are always One:
'Our tents are apart, our hearts are one.'
Oneness of vision converts the motes to the sun;
be one of vision, that God may be seen unveiled.
Do not look slightingly on oneness of vision;
this is a true epiphany of the Unity.
When a nation becomes drunk with the Unity
power, yea, omnipotence lies in its grasp.

A nation's spirit exists through association;
a nation's spirit has no need of a body.
Since its being manifests out of companionship,
it dies when the bands of companionship are broken.
Are you dead? Become living through oneness of vision;
cease to be centreless, become stable.
Create unity of thought and action,
that you may possess authority in the world.

Zinda-Rud

Who am I? Who art Thou? Where is the world?
Why is there a distance between me and Thee?

Say, why am I in the bonds of destiny?
Why dost Thou die not, whilst I die?

The Voice of Beauty

You have been in the world dimensionate,
and any contained therein, therein dies.
If you seek life, advance your selfhood,
drown the world's dimensions in your self.
You shall then behold who I am and who you are
how you died in the world, and how you lived.

Zinda-Rud

Accept the excuses of this ignorant man;
remove the veil from the face of destiny.
I have seen the revolution of Russia and Germany,
I have seen the tumult raging in Moslemdom,
I have seen the contrivings of West and East—
prevent the destinies of West and East.

Epiphany of the Divine Majesty

Suddenly I beheld my world,
that earth and heaven of mine,
I saw it drowned in a light of dawn;
I saw it crimson as a jujube-tree:
out of the epiphanies which broke in my soul
I fell drunk with ecstasy, like Moses.
That light revealed every secret veiled
and snatched the power of speech from my tongue.
Out of the deep heart of the inscrutable world
an ardent, flaming melody broke forth.

'Abandon the East, be not spellbound by the West,
for all this ancient and new is not worth one barleycorn.

That signet-ring which you gambled away to Ahriman
should not be pledged even to trusty Gabriel.
Life, that ornament of society, is guardian of itself;
you who are of the caravan, travel alone, yet go with all!
You have come forth brighter than the all-illumining sun;
so live, that you may irradiate every mote.
Alexander, Darius, Qubad and Khusrau have departed
like a blade of grass fallen in the path of the wind.
So slender is your cup that the tavern has been put to shame;
seize a tumbler, and drink wisely, and so be gone!'

NOTES

31. 'The Verse of Subjection': Koran XXXI 19:

    Have you not seen how that God has subjected to you whatsoever is in the the heavens and earth?

33. See Koran II 29, telling of the creation of Adam:

    And He taught Adam the names, all of them.

38. Koran XL 62:

    Your Lord has said, 'Call upon Me
    and I will answer you.'

77. 'The Samiri': the one who persuaded the Israelites to worship the Golden Calf, see Koran XX 87.

90. Koran II 182:

    And when My servants question thee
    concerning Me—I am near to answer
    the call of the caller, when he calls
    to Me.

141. Alvand is a high mountain near Hamadan in Persia.

181. 'This precious subject': Man, as the darling object of God's thought. This phrase is interpreted variously by the different translators.

199. Iqbal introduces verses from a famous ode by the Persian mystic Jalal al-Din Rumi, inserting into it lines of his own (verses 205–6). For the whole poem see R. A. Nicholson, *Selected Poems from the Divani Shamsi Tabriz* (Cambridge, 1898), no. XVI.

208. Oman was the name given to the southernmost stretch of the Persian Gulf.

214. 'The Lion of God' was a title given to the Prophet Mohammed's cousin and son-in-law Ali, fourth caliph of Islam. Rustam-i Dastan, Rustam son of Zal (nicknamed Dastan after his cunning), was a famous hero of pre-Islamic Persia, familiar to Western readers from Matthew Arnold's poem *Sohrab and Rustum.*

220. 'Like a witness': the original can also mean (and perhaps this alternative is preferable) 'like a beautiful one'.

237. 'The day primordial': literally, 'the Day of Alast ("Am I not?")' as described in Koran VII 171:

    And when thy Lord took from the Children of Adam,
    from their loins, their seed, and made them testify
    touching themselves, 'Am I not your Lord?'
    They said, 'Yes, we testify'.

271. 'The Authority': see next note.

277. Iqbal refers to Koran LV 33:

> O tribe of jinn and of men, if you are able to
> pass through the confines of heaven and earth,
> pass through them! You shall not pass through
> except with an authority.

285. The contrast is between predestination and freewill.

296. Iqbal refers to the Moslem practice of whispering the Call to Prayer into the ear of the new-born baby at the naming ceremony.

331. Khaibar was a Jewish settlement and stronghold, a hundred miles from Medina, which was conquered with miraculous ease in AD 628.

332. The reference is to the famous miracle of 'the splitting of the moon' recounted in explanation of Koran LIV 1:

> The Hour has drawn nigh: the moon is split.

333. Refers to Abraham's victory over Nimrod as described in Koran XXI 68–9. Moslem legend tells of how a mosquito entered Nimrod's nostril and penetrated his brain, thus killing him.

334. The destruction of Pharaoh and his hosts in the Red Sea is described in Koran XXVI 60–65.

359. Here and at lines 363–6 Iqbal quotes from the *Masnavi* of Rumi.

393. Zarvan: for a full discussion of the role of this figure in Zoroastrianism, see R. C. Zaehner, *Zurvan, a Zoroastrian dilemma.*

425. Iqbal refers to a well-known saying of Mohammed: 'I have a time with God, in which none of the cherubim nor any prophet rivals me'; see R. A. Nicholson, *The Kashf al-Mahjúb*, p. 368.

460 'The Samiri': see note on verse 77.

465. The breaking of Alexander's legendary rampart will portend the end of the world; see Koran XVIII 91 ff., XXI 96.

505. Imaginary names for mountains of the moon.

529. Jahan-Dost ('Friend of the World') is to be identified with Vishvamitra, the teacher of Rama in Hindu legend.

591. Another imaginary mountain of the moon.

598. Iqbal has in mind the story of Harut and Marut (see Koran II 96), two fallen angels condemned (their sin was falling in love with the daughters of men) to inhabit a well at Babylon.

605. Azar, the father of Abraham, was an idolator; see Koran VI 74.

637. Iqbal has in mind the saying of Mohammed, 'We have returned from the lesser Holy War to the greater Holy War'; the latter is commonly explained as 'the struggle with the carnal soul'.

679. Sarosh in the Mazdean religion was an angel-personification of obedience.

689. Razi: Fakhr al-Din al-Razi (*d.* AD 1210), celebrated theologian and philosopher, composed many books including a great commentary on the Koran, which Iqbal rejects because of its alleged Peripatetic tendencies.

696. Iqbal has in mind a popular mystical poem which includes the line: 'He is in me, and I am in Him, like scent in rose-water.'

701. Yarghamid is yet another imaginary lunar place-name. Tawasin is the Arabic plural of Tasin, a mysterious symbol prefixed to Koran XXVII. The celebrated mystic-martyr Hallaj, executed on a charge of blasphemy in AD 922, wrote a book entitled 'The Book of Tawasin.'

702. Salsabil is a fountain in Paradise.

704. 'He is God': Koran CXII reversed, chanted by ecstatic mystics.

710. 'The Trusty Spirit': Gabriel.

713. Iqbal criticizes the effeminate style of the later Persian poets of India.

716. Abraham was called 'the friend of God'; all good Moslems may be called the like.

731. 'His signs': evidentiary proof of the genuineness of the prophet's mission.

738. Iqbal names the titles of Suras LIII, XXIV and LXXIX of the Koran.

793. Iqbal refers to the famous story of Farhad, who dug his way through a mountain to reach his beloved Shirin.

800. The 'White Hand' first manifested in Moses (see Koran XX 23) is a symbol of the miraculous power of prophets.

804. All prophets and saints are 'tried' by God. The saw symbolizes Zachariah, the worm Job, the cross Jesus.

872. Ifrangin is coined as the spirit of the corrupted Christian civilization of Europe.

907. Abu Jahl, a stubborn enemy of Mohammed, was killed at the Battle of Badr in AD 623.

915. Lat and Manat were ancient idols of Arabia.

926. Koraish was a noble tribe to which Mohammed belonged.

934. Salman 'the Persian' was an ardent companion of Mohammed. The Mazdakites were adherents of the Persian heresiarch Mazdak.

935. Mohammed's father was named Abdullah.

937. Hashim was an ancestor of Mohammed, founder of the clan to which he belonged.

939. Adnan was the eponymous founder of a large Arab group of tribes, hence legendary ancestor of the Arab people.

940. Sahban was a famous Arab orator.

942. Zuhair was a celebrated pre-Islamic Arab poet.

945. The Black Stone is housed in the Kaaba at Mecca.

947. Hubal was an idol worshipped by the pagan Arabs.

952. This line is a quotation from Koran LXIX 7.

953. See note on verse 925.

956. Iqbal quotes from a verse of the great pre-Islamic Arab poet Imra' al-Qais.

957. Jamal al-Din Afghani (*c.* 1838–1897) was one of the leading figures in the nineteenth-century revivalist movement, a pioneer of Moslem unity. Sa'id Halim Pasha (1838–1914), prominent Ottoman statesman, also preached Pan-Islam.

987. Fudail (*d.* AD 803) was a famous ascetic. Bu Sa'id (*d.* AD 1049) was a pioneer of Persian mystical poetry.

988. Junaid (*d.* AD 910) was a central figure in the Baghdad school of 'sober' mystics. Bu Yazid (*d. c.* 877) was a leader of the Khorasanian 'intoxicated' school.

992. Iqbal refers to Sa'id Halim Pasha and Jamal al-Din Afghani respectively.

997. Maulana is a title of respect equivalent to 'the Master'. Sayyids are those who claim descent from Mohammed.

1004. 'The Chapter of the Star' is Koran LIII.

1012. 'The Heavenly Archetype' is the original of the Koran laid up in Heaven.

1020. Zinda-Rud, 'Living Stream', is the name of the river on which Isfahan stands, and of any great river. From this point Iqbal refers to himself as Zinda-Rud.

1036. Iqbal attacks the post-1918 settlement of the Arab world, a settlement imposed by the 'Western Lord' statesmen. In verse 1064 he extends his condemnation of the 'fragmentation' of Moslem Unity to include Iran, Egypt and Yemen.

1070. 'That prophet': Karl Marx.

1117. Mustafa Kemal, calling himself Atatürk, founder of the modern Turkish nation, died AD 1938, admired elsewhere in Iqbal's poetry as a champion of the revival of the East, is here criticized for adopting Western ideas of nationhood.

1150. Omar, second caliph of Islam, was converted suddenly from being a stubborn opponent into being a leading champion of Mohammed.

1163. The quotation is from Koran II 28:

> And when thy Lord said to the angels,
> 'I am setting in the earth a viceroy'.

1205. Mount Hira is a hill near Mecca to which Mohammed used to withdraw to meditate.

1223. God's answer to Moses when he prayed for the Beatific Vision, see Koran VII 138.

1283. In a number of passages in the Koran, earthly possessions are termed an 'enjoyment' (or 'usufruct') for man, see for example Koran VII 23.

1291. Based upon such texts as Koran XLV 26:

> To God belongs the Kingdom of the heavens and the earth.

1309. Based upon Koran II 272:

> He gives the Wisdom to whomsoever He will,
> and whoso is given the Wisdom, has been
> given much good.

1346. Abu Lahab was one of Mohammed's most bitter enemies, and is named in malediction in Koran CXI 1. Haidar is a nickname of Ali, for whom see note on line 214.

1360. See note on line 710.

1378. Like Moses in Koran XX 23. The 'white' people in verse 1385 are those who have shared in the miracle of the White Hand.

1381. 'The Chosen One': Mustafa, a nickname of Mohammed.

1386. Here and in verse 1394 Iqbal is thinking of Koran LV 29:

> Every day He is upon some labour.

For Iqbal's views on the philosophical implications of this text, see his *Reconstruction of Religious Thought in Islam*, p. 48.

1394. A famous saying of Mohammed. In Urdu, the word *gharib* (stranger) also means 'poor'.

1432. The 'days' of the Arabs were their famous victories, and, by extension, the triumphant spread of Islam.

1438. Refers to the Moslem credo, 'There is *no* god *but* God'.

1444. See note on line 1012.

1445. See note on line 1378.

1466. Iqbal quotes Koran III 86.

1468. See Koran II 246:

> Who is he that will lend God a good loan,
> and He will multiply it for him manifold?

1474. See Koran XXVIII 88:

> All things perish, except His Face.

1476. Iqbal has in mind Koran XXVII 34:

> Kings, when they enter a city, disorder it.

1478. Koran XXXI 27:

> Your creation and your upraising are as
> but a single soul.

1489. See Koran IX 112.

1490. See Koran II 216–17.

1522. The leader of a caravan urges on the camels by singing.

1526. As ordered by Nimrod, see Koran XXXVII 95.

1540. 'Without sweetmeats and boon-companion': the regular accompaniment to the wine as symbol of spiritual fervour.

1556. Abraham's son, whom God commanded Abraham to sacrifice and then spared, see Koran XXXVII 100–109.

1557. See note on line 331.

1558. See note on line 1346.

1563. See Koran LIII 17.

1570. Zain al-Abidin was the grandson of Ali, son of Husain, almost sole survivor of his family at the Battle of Kerbela in AD 680.

1620. Khizr, a mysterious figure in Moslem legend, acted as guide to Alexander in his quest for the Water of Immortality.

1629. 'The Beautiful Name': Allah.

1630. Abraham, stated in the Koran to have been the builder of the Kaaba at Mecca, is represented as the first great champion of monotheism against idolatry.

1651. Alast: see note on verse 237.

1657. The charge is that the Moslem has turned dualist.

1704. Kitchener's death in 1916 aboard H.M.S. *Hampshire* is seen as retribution for his repression of the Mahdists in the Sudan, culminating in the Battle of Omdurman in 1898.

1717. 'The Sura of Taha': Koran XX, in which the story of Moses and Pharaoh is recounted at length.

1738. Iqbal has in mind the saying *divide et impera*.

1741. 'God's interlocutor': the title by which Moses is known.

1758. Referring to the charge that Lord Kitchener ordered the disinterment of the Sudanese Mahdi and the scattering of his bones.

1773. The then kings of Egypt, Iraq and Saoudi Arabia.

1777. Batha is the name of the valley of Mecca. Khalid (*d.* 641–2) was a famous general of the Moslem conquests.

1780. This verse is a compliment to the then Prince Farouk of Egypt. Farouk was a title given to the second caliph Omar.

1789. Yathrib: the ancient name of Medina.

1825. See note on verse 1620.

1866. Merv: a city once lying within Persian Khorasan, now part of USSR.

1870. Tusi, Persian polymath, died in 1274. His most famous book, the *Akhlaq-i Nasiri*, was composed in Persian.

1903. Barkhiya is incidentally the name given to the father of Asaf, King Solomon's minister.

2000. Iqbal quotes Koran II 10, VII 54.

2099. For Hallaj, see note on verse 701. Ghalib (1797–1869) was the greatest Persian poet of India in his times. Qurrat al-Ain, Persian poetess and martyr of the Babi movement, was executed in 1852.

2145. Naziri (*d.* 1612) was a famous Persian poet born in Nishapur who passed most of his active life in India. Jamshid was one of the greatest kings of ancient Persia.

2150. Sulaima is a symbol of the beloved.

2331. See note on verse 1777.

2237. Iqbal quotes from Rumi's *Masnavi*, V 3356 ff. For Ba Yazid, see note on verse 998.

2254. Iqbal refers to Koran VIII 17, the context of which is the Battle of Badr:

> You did not slay them, but God slew them;
> and when thou threwest, it was not
> thyself that threw, but God threw.

2263. 'God's bidding': a reference to Koran XVII 87:

> They will question thee concerning
> the Spirit. Say: 'The Spirit is of
> the bidding of my Lord.'

2272. It was on Sinai (Koran VII 139) that Moses witnessed the effects of the Divine epiphany.

2303. Mani, the founder of Manicheeism, was a miraculous painter.

2314. Iqbal quotes Koran XXI 107.

2321. Iqbal has in mind Koran LXXXVIII 2–3.

2339. Iqbal here develops the mystical doctrine of the Idea of Mohammed as an archetypal Spirit and 'the medium through which God becomes conscious of Himself in creation' (R. A. Nicholson, *Studies in Islamic Mysticism*, p. 110).

2362. Koran VIII 17.

2367. 'The Last of Time': Mohammed as the Seal of the Prophets.

2372. The Sunna is the model way of life as exemplified by the acts of Mohammed.

2407. Iblis as reported in Koran VII 11. For the role of Satan in Islamic mysticism, especially the doctrine of Hallaj, see R. A. Nicholson, *The Idea of Personality in Sufism*, p. 31

2496. Iqbal quotes a well-known Tradition of Mohammed, primarily meant as a disincentive to divorce.

2561. Two Indian generals who accepted service in the East India Company during the expansion of British dominion.

2618. Iqbal quotes from Koran XXXVI 25.

2624. 'The templars': the Brahmins.

2626. Antar, heroic warrior and poet of ancient Arabia, is here contrasted as a pagan with the true type of hero, Ali.

2629. For Iqbal's attitude to Nietzsche, see his *Reconstruction of Religious Thought*, p. 184.

2738. See note on line 1438.

2746. As in Koran VII 139.

2747. Ahmad: Ahmad Sirhindi (1564–1624), eminent Indian theologian known as 'the Renovator of the Second Millennium'.

2805. Kauthar is a river in Paradise.

2809. Sharaf al-Nisa Begum was the granddaughter of Abd al-Samad Khan, governor of Panjab in the early years of the eighteenth century.

2855. 'The Khalsa': the Sikhs.

2857. Sayyid Ali Hamadani (*d.* 1385) was a famous Persian mystic who lived his later years in Kashmir. Mulla Tahir Ghani (*d.* 1669) was an eminent poet of Kashmir.

2863. Iqbal quotes a couplet from Tahir Ghani.

2873. Ghazali (*d.* 1111), most eminent theologian and mystic of Persia.

2877. 'That vale': Kashmir.

2929. Nishat is a famous garden in Srinagar.

2930. Iqbal quotes the opening words of Rumi's *Masnavi*.

2934. Nauruz is the new year's day festival in Persia.

2938. Shihab al-Din, the greatest of the Ghorid kings of India, died in 1206.

2951. Iqbal refers to the sale of Kashmir under the 1846 Treaty of Amritsar, a settlement which still embitters relations between Pakistan and India.

2986. The best-known book written by Ali Hamadani is entitled 'The Treasury of Kings', a treatise on statecraft.

2993. Koran IV 62:

> O believers, obey God, and obey the Messenger
> and those in authority among you.

3001. King Jamshid of ancient Persia is said to have possessed a magic cup in which the entire world was mirrored, thus becoming a symbol for royal power.

3020. Wular is a lake in Kashmir.

3070. Rustam-i Dastan: see note on line 214. 'Magian boys' were the wine-bearers in Magian taverns, here types of effeminacy.

3078. Badakhshan was famous as a source of rubies.

3079. Bartari-Hari or Bhartrihari, a Hindu poet of the seventh century, is renowned for his Sanskrit epigrams.

3090. Azar is the sixth of the Syrian months, corresponding with March, the season of spring rains.

3117. Iqbal states that this sequence of verses were a translation from Bhartrihari.

3135. Nadir Shah (*d.* 1747), great conqueror and founder of the short-lived Afsharid dynasty of Persia, for a time ruled from Caucasus to the Indus.

3137. Abdali: Ahmad Shah Durrani (*d.* 1773) founded the modern nation of Afghanistan.

3139. 'The Martyr-King' was Tippoo Sultan of Mysore (*d.* 1799).

3145. The battles of Badr and Hunain were two of Mohammed's famous victories.

3146. Husain, son of the fourth caliph Ali, was killed at the Battle of Kerbela in AD 680.

3172. Bahram, 'that great Hunter', a hero of Sassanid Persia.

3188. Shapur was the name of three Persian kings.

3195. Yazdajird III (*d.* 651 or 652) was the last of the Sassanid kings of Persia, defeated by the conquering armies of Islam.

3212. Nasir-i Khusrau (*d.* 1060 or 1061) was one of the greatest of the early Persian poets.

3223. 'That youth': the Afghan people.

3237. Khushhal Khan Khatak (*d.* 1691), warrior and poet, is the most famous figure in Pashto literature.

3277. 'The antidote of Iraq': a drug famous as a specific against poisons.

3308. Iqbal compliments the rulers of Iran and Afghanistan.

3309. Qubad was an ancient king of Persia.

3311. The Durranis are the ruling house of Afghanistan.

3345. The Cauvery is the principal river of Mysore, running through Tippoo Sultan's old capital city of Seringapatam (see line 3371).

3370. 'The Water of Life': the legendary river sought by Alexander.

3436. Allahu Akbar: 'God is Most Great', the Moslem battlecry.

3438. Murtada's son: Husain, for whom see note on verse 3146. Murtada is one of the titles of Ali.

3444. Iqbal refers to a famous saying of Mohammed.

3577. Koran II 182.

3581. For Ba Yazid, see note on line 988. Shibli (*d.* 945) was a noted mystic of Baghdad. Bu Dharr was a Companion of Mohammed famous for his piety.

3582. Tughril (*d.* 1063) was the first of the Seljuk rulers of medieval Islam. Sanjar (*d.* 1157) was the last of the great Seljuks.

3587. For Salman, see the note on line 934.

BIBLIOGRAPHY

A splendidly extensive and detailed bibliography of Iqbal and Iqbal studies is appended to A. Schimmel, *Gabriel's Wing* (Leiden, 1963) and to this the student may confidently turn. The list below represents a selection of works bearing more particularly on the translation and interpretation of the *Jovid-nama*.

TEXT

IQBAL, *Javid-nama*. Lahore, 1932. With Persian–Urdu glossary, Hyderabad (Deccan), 1946.

TRANSLATIONS

A. BAUSANI, *Il Poema Celeste*. Rome, 1952.

A. SCHIMMEL, *Buch der Ewigkeit*. Munich, 1957.

MAHMUD AHMAD, *The Pilgrimoge of Eternity*. Lahore, 1961.

E. MEYEROVITCH and MOHAMMED MOKRI, *Le Livre de l'Éternité*. Paris, 1962.

BIOGRAPHIES

A. ANWAR BEG, *The Poet of the Eost*. Lahore, 1939.

IQBAL SINGH, *The Ardent Pilgrim*. London, 1951.

STUDIES

Aspects of Iqbol (various authors). Lahore, 1938.

B. A. DAR, *A Study in Iqbal's Philosophy*. Lahore, 1944.

I. H. ENVER, *The Metophysics of Iqbal*. Lahore, 1944.

S. A. VAHID, *Iqbal, his Art ond Thought*. Lahore, 1944 (enlarged edition, London, 1959).

Iqbol os o Thinker (various authors). Lahore, 1945.

K. G. SAIYIDAIN, *Iqbol's Educotionol Philosophy*. Lahore, 1945.

S. SINHA, *Iqbal, the Poet ond his Message*. Allahabad, 1947.

A. SCHIMMEL, *Gobriel's Wing*. Leiden, 1963.

OTHER TRANSLATIONS

R. A. NICHOLSON, *Secrets of the Self*. London, 1920.

A. J. ARBERRY, *Tulip of Sinai*. London, 1947.

V. G. KIERNAN, *Poems from Iqbal*. Bombay, 1947 (new edition, London, 1955).

A. J. ARBERRY, *Persion Psolms*. Lahore, 1948.

A. J. ARBERRY, *Mysteries of Selflessness*. London, 1953.

www.ingramcontent.com/pod-product-compliance
Ingram Content Group UK Ltd.
Pitfield, Milton Keynes, MK11 3LW, UK
UKHW021407190726
13845UKWH00028B/935

9 789366 084190